THE GOLDEN BOOK
IRELAND

Text by
FRANCES POWER

Photographs by
GHIGO ROLI

O'BRIEN
DUBLIN

B BONECHI

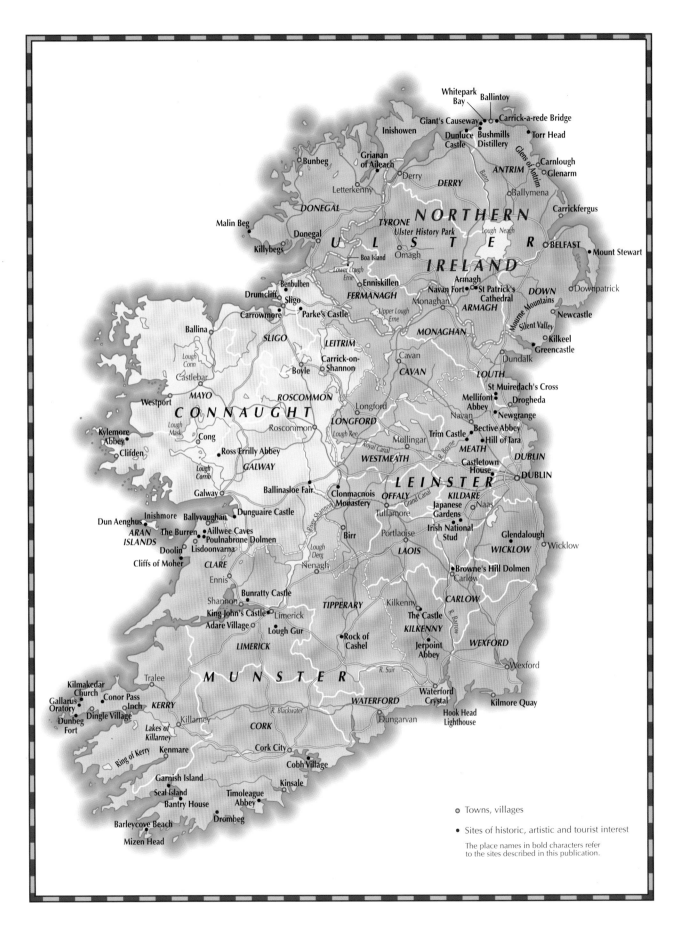

Whitepark Bay Ballintoy
Giant's Causeway Carrick-a-rede Bridge
Inishowen Dunluce Bushmills Torr Head
Castle Distillery
Bunbeg Grianan Carnlough
of Aileach Glenarm
Derry DERRY ANTRIM
Letterkenny Ballymena
DONEGAL NORTHERN Carrickfergus
Malin Beg TYRONE ULSTER
Donegal Ulster History Park Lough Neagh BELFAST
Killybegs Boa Island Omagh IRELAND Mount Stewart
Lower Lough Armagh DOWN Downpatrick
Erne Enniskillen Navan Fort St Patrick's
Benbulben FERMANAGH Monaghan Cathedral
Drumcliff Sligo Upper Lough ARMAGH Mourne Mountains Newcastle
Carrowmore Parke's Castle Erne MONAGHAN Silent Valley Kilkeel
Ballina Greencastle
SLIGO LEITRIM Dundalk
Carrick-on- Cavan LOUTH
Boyle Shannon CAVAN St Muiredach's Cross
Castlebar Longford Mellifont Drogheda
MAYO ROSCOMMON Abbey Newgrange
Westport CONNAUGHT LONGFORD Navan Bective Abbey
Roscommon Lough Ree Trim Castle Hill of Tara
Kylemore Lough MEATH
Abbey Mask Mullingar Castletown DUBLIN
Clifden Cong Royal Canal WESTMEATH House DUBLIN
Ross Errilly Abbey LEINSTER
Lough Clonmacnois KILDARE
Corrib Ballinasloe Fair Monastery Japanese Naas
Galway GALWAY Tullamore OFFALY Gardens
Inishmore Dunguaire Castle Grand Canal Irish National Glendalough
Dun Aenghus Ballyvaughan Birr Portlaoise Stud Wicklow
ARAN The Burren Aillwee Caves River Shannon WICKLOW
ISLANDS Poulnabrone Dolmen Lough LAOIS Browne's Hill Dolmen
Doolin Lisdoonvarna Derg Carlow
Cliffs of Moher CLARE Nenagh CARLOW
Ennis Kilkenny R. Barrow
Bunratty Castle TIPPERARY The Castle
Shannon KILKENNY WEXFORD
King John's Castle Limerick Rock of Jerpoint
Adare Village Lough Gur Cashel Abbey Wexford
LIMERICK R. Suir
MUNSTER WATERFORD Waterford Kilmore Quay
Kilmakedar Tralee Crystal
Church Conor Pass KERRY Hook Head Lighthouse
Gallarus Inch R. Blackwater Dungarvan
Oratory Dingle Village Killarney CORK
Dunbeg Lakes of Cork City
Fort Killarney
Ring of Kerry Kenmare Cobh Village
Garnish Island Kinsale
Seal Island Timoleague
Bantry House Abbey
Barleycove Beach Drombeg
Mizen Head

o Towns, villages

• Sites of historic, artistic and tourist interest

The place names in bold characters refer
to the sites described in this publication.

INTRODUCTION

*I*reland has had a turbulent history with wave after wave of settlers, each leaving their mark on the landscape in the shape of megaliths, monasteries, castles or great country houses. First came hunter-gatherers in about 6000BC, followed by Stone Age farmers who cleared land and cultivated the soil and left behind great stone monuments and the many dolmens and stone circles that are sprinkled around the country. With the Bronze Age, around 1500BC, came an increasing sophistication in construction – the awe-inspiring forts of Dun Aengus on Inishmore and Grianán of Aileach in Donegal date from this period. Roughly a thousand years later the Celts arrived in Ireland from Central Europe. They lived in defensive structures such as ring forts, raths and crannógs of which over thirty thousand remain. Their skill in metalworking is to be seen in the beautiful bronze pieces on show in the National Museum in Dublin. Under the Celts Ireland was divided into five provinces of which Ulster, Munster, Leinster and Connaught still survive. Each province was broken up into many small kingdoms ruled over by a chieftain, and all were, supposedly, under the rule of a High King who, according to myth, reigned from Tara in County Meath.

In 432AD St Patrick arrived, other missionaries soon followed, and gradually Christianity seeped into pagan Ireland. While Europe was suffering the chaos of the Dark Ages, Ireland was becoming a centre of Christianity and scholarship. Missionaries such as St Columcille went to Europe, some to set up schools and universities. Many of Ireland's monastic sites date from this period, the most notable were Clonmacnois on the Shannon, Glendalough in Co Wicklow, and Kells, where the stunning Book of Kells may have been penned. These monasteries held great treasures – intricately worked gold shrines and, of course, illuminated manuscripts. And it was the promise of treasures such as these that lured the next wave of invaders, the Vikings, to Ireland at the end of the 8th century. Their arrival also sparked the first attempt at a unified Irish defence. At the Battle of Clontarf in 1014, Brian Boru, High King of Ireland, led an alliance of Gaelic chiefs against the Norsemen. They scored a decisive victory. Those Vikings who did not flee, married into the Irish and, for a few years at least, there was peace.

Then a squabble in 1169 led the deposed Dermot MacMurrough, King of Leinster, to turn to Henry II of England for help in regaining his kingdom. In response, Henry sent Richard FitzGilbert de Clare, known as Strongbow, with his Anglo-Norman forces to Ireland and the first stages of English rule began.

One of the many dolmens constructed by Stone Age settlers.

Strongbow married MacMurrough's daughter Aoife and eventually became King of Leinster, establishing the Anglo-Normans firmly in power. By the 15th century, despite the best efforts of English monarchs and the passing of the Statutes of Kilkenny, forbidding intermarriage, the speaking of Irish or wearing of Irish costume, the Anglo-Normans were well-integrated into Gaelic culture and the sphere of English influence had shrunk to a tiny area around Dublin known as 'the Pale'.

It was not until the reign of Elizabeth I that the power of the Gaelic chieftains was permanently crushed. The most telling defeat was that of the Ulster earls at the Battle of Kinsale in 1601. Some years later, in what became known as 'the Flight of the Earls', the great Ulster chiefs O'Neill and O'Donnell left Ireland with a large retinue and sailed for the Continent, signalling the end of the Gaelic aristocracy's rule in Ireland. The subsequent power vacuum – and the fact that large tracts of land formerly belonging to these Gaels were confiscated by the Crown – left the way open for wide-scale plantation of Ulster, mainly by Scottish Presbyterians and English settlers. When the native Catholic Irish were driven off the land to make way for the settlers, the seeds were sown for the conflict that still tears Northern Ireland apart.

In the 1640s Oliver Cromwell turned his attention from the Civil War in England to an Irish rebellion which was put down with a thoroughness that was unprecedented. By the 1660s, devastated by Cromwell's massacres, and the plague and famine that followed, only 500,000 native Irish remained. A series of acts known as the Penal Laws then completed the submission of the Irish Catholics and Dissenters, restricting religious practice, culture, property ownership and power. For the next century it would be up to the Protestant Anglo-Irish, who had been experiencing a remarkable prosperity and consequent confidence, to seek some measure of independence from colonial rule.

In 1782 the Anglo-Irish ruling class achieved a virtually independent parliament in Dublin, and the worst of the Penal Laws were also repealed. However, in 1798, influenced by the French Revolution, the United Irishmen rebellion began. It was shortlived and unsuccessful. In response, the Act of Union was passed in 1800 amalgamating the Irish parliament with that at Westminster in London, and effectively ending Irish independence.

The Irish peasantry then suffered another devastating blow. From 1845-1849 the potato crops failed. Two-thirds of the country survived on this staple, and its failure led to famine on an unimaginable scale, reducing the population from 8 million to 4 million by 1851 through emigration, disease and starvation.

Despite the devastation, nationalist movements continued to grow in strength during the 19th century. And it was the growth of mass movements such as the Land League and the Home Rule movement – which united the various strands of nationalism to bring pressure to bear on the English government – that signalled the growth of a cohesive national identity.

In 1912, against great opposition from Ulster Protestants, a Home Rule Bill was finally passed. But World War I intervened before the act could be implemented and Irishmen from both north and south enlisted in large numbers to fight for England. In 1916 another rising took place. Under Eamon de Valera a provisional government was set up in Dublin with Michael Collins heading the military wing and the War of Independence began.

Facing page, top, left, a Janus stone dating from pagan Ireland, and bottom, some Irish myths and legends, including those about fairies and leprechauns, are believed to date from the same period.

This page, each period in Irish history has left its mark on the landscape, top, right, the 6th century monastery at Glendalough in County Wicklow, and bottom, Jerpoint Abbey in County Kilkenny, which dates from the 12th century.

In 1920 the Government of Ireland Act created separate parliaments for the South, comprising the twenty-six counties of today's Republic, and the North, containing the six counties of Antrim, Tyrone, Derry, Down, Armagh and Fermanagh. A peace treaty was negotiated with the British by Michael Collins, among others, but de Valera's dissatisfaction with its terms led to civil war. Peace was eventually agreed, but only after bitter fighting.

In 1937 de Valera presented the constitution that has safeguarded Ireland's civil rights ever since and, in 1948, Ireland – minus the six counties – was declared a Republic.

In the North, after Partition, power had remained largely in Protestant hands, and discrimination against Catholics was widespread, particularly in jobs and housing. In 1968 civil rights marchers took to the streets demanding equal rights. The marchers were attacked by loyalist mobs, and riots broke out. The British army was sent in initially to defend the Catholic minority, but events escalated – in 1971 a policy of internment without trial was introduced, in 1972, in what became known as Bloody Sunday, British paratroopers shot and killed thirteen unarmed civil rights marchers. The Provisional IRA launched a bombing campaign killing and maiming many hundreds. In response loyalist paramilitary organisations carried out killings. In recent times, hope of a settlement has appeared – a ceasefire in 1994 brought 'talks about talks' between the British and Irish government and the various parties involved. While that ceasefire ended with an IRA bomb in London, a new ceasefire came into being in 1997 and hope still exists that a settlement may eventually be agreed.

In 1991 with the election of constitutional lawyer Mary Robinson to President, the Republic of Ireland seemed to come of age. One of the by-products was a renewed interest in Irish culture and language. Another was a new spirit of liberalism which led to the legalisation of divorce in 1996 and a referendum that removed a ban on information about abortion services – though abortion remains illegal. This liberalising attitude is partly the result of the economic boom which means young people no longer have to emigrate in search of work and, consequently, have a voice in running the country. It may also be partly due to an increasing integration into Western Europe. Whatever the reasons, the results are clear – a rapidly changing society, driven by a strong economy and a highly-trained young workforce.

Some things don't change, however. Ireland is still a country with a rich and unique culture, best expressed in music and storytelling and, most of all, the art of conversation.

The modern face of Dublin, the International Financial Services Centre.

Climate and Flora

*I*rish weather changes constantly, and it is quite normal to experience many different climates in one day. The warm currents of the Gulf Stream and prevailing westerly winds blowing in from the Atlantic, however, guarantee mild winters and cool summers, with lots of rain and wind and an average temperature of 9°-10.5°C. And since Ireland sits in the middle latitudes with only four degrees difference between north and south it lacks extremes of weather.

Even so it is possible to distinguish slight differences between regions – the northwest is windier and wetter than, for example, the southeast, which boasts the most hours of sunshine.

The topography too is one of contrasts and provides a range of habitats for flora. In the west the limestone plateau of the Burren yields rare species of plant more often found in Mediterranean and Alpine-Arctic conditions. The coastline is sprinkled with sand dunes, particularly in Wexford, Donegal, Kerry and Mayo, which come alive in summer with wild flowers such as orchid and bird's foot trefoil. Inland, the abundance of rain and poor drainage has led to marshes and wetlands filled with reeds, fen violet, water germander, stone bramble and dewberry, while tracts of bogland in the midlands produce heather, bog cotton, bog myrtle and a variety of grasses.

Top, right, Irish weather can change from minute to minute, bottom, left and right, and its mildness produces a surprising range of flora.

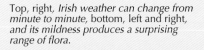

Economy and local industry

The years since 1993 have been golden ones for the Republic's economy. Unemployment has fallen, inflation is at an all time low, and growth rates are equal to those of some of the most competitive countries in the world. New industries, both foreign and domestic, are sprouting up, particularly in the electronics and communications industries – Ireland is now the biggest producer of computer software in Europe. The picture in the North has not been so bright. Badly hit by 'the Troubles', the North depends heavily on the British government's investment into what has been, traditionally, a more industrial economy with shipbuilding and the linen industry at its core. However, since 1994 and the first of the ceasefires, the number of tourists visiting the North has grown, and a new sense of confidence in the peace process is drawing increasing numbers of foreign investors.

Up until recently Ireland was predominantly an agricultural country and dairy and cattle farming were, and still are, important. Joining the European Community in 1972 brought greater profits to farmers and there was an agricultural boom. Through the 1980s and early 90s, however, falling prices, recession and the lure of urban living have drawn increasing numbers from the land – 39 percent of the Republic's population of 3.6 million now live on the urbanised east coast. At the same time, a change of economic direction on the part of the government brought foreign investment to Ireland with tax breaks, grant schemes and employment incentives. These multinationals still account for a large proportion of gross domestic product.

Tourism is another of the country's largest employers with 107,000 working in the industry, bringing in £1,445 billion in revenue annually, a figure which is growing at a rate of 12 percent per year. A new wave of craftsworkers, artists, weavers, potters, jewellery-makers have settled in the more remote areas of the country such as Kerry, West Cork, Connemara and Donegal, and produce fine examples of Irish handcrafts for sale to tourists. Another important industry is fishing – and few visitors to Ireland leave without having tasted smoked salmon, Dublin Bay prawns, oysters or mussels.

Traditional music is a growing export – as far back as

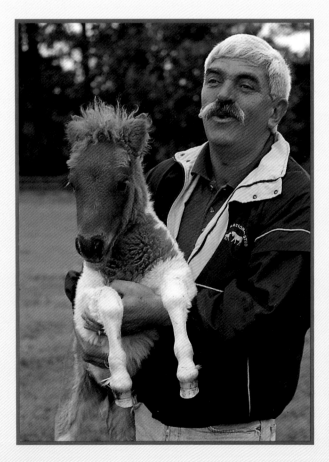

the 1970s traditional music began to experience a renaissance with the fusion of rock and traditional that typified the groups Planxty and Moving Hearts. Now musicians such as Van Morrison and Sinead O'Connor reinvent the old airs and add new ones, while traditional musicians refresh their music with influences and instruments from as far afield as Africa and Australia. In other areas of Irish music other talents, such as U2, Enya, Clannad, the Cranberries and Boyzone, are dominating music headlines.

Other newer industries are culturally-based – in 1993 the Irish Film Board was reconstituted, and a special tax investment scheme put in place. The results were immediate – a vibrant film industry is now established, with both well-known Irish filmmakers such as Neil Jordan, Jim Sheridan and Noel Pearson, as well as talented newcomers producing award-winning films and demonstrating that the ancient tradition of storytelling is alive and well and expressing itself in a new medium.

Traditional industries such as horse-breeding and fishing, facing page, bottom, left and right, *still exist alongside handcrafts,* this page, *such as pottery, jewellery-making and the ever-popular Aran jumper.*

DUBLIN

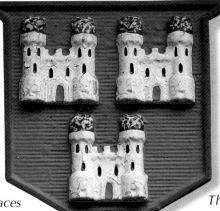

Dublin sits in a vast natural harbour that stretches from Howth in the north to Dalkey in the south. It is bisected by the River Liffey which flows through the city and out into Dublin Bay. Such a sheltered harbour would have appealed to the first settlers 5,000 years ago and traces of their culture have been found scattered around Dublin and its coast. But it was not until the Vikings came sailing down the east coast in the mid 9th century that Dublin became an important town. Next to arrive were the Anglo-Norman adventurers sent by Henry II of England in 1169 in response to a petition for arms from Dermot MacMurrough, the deposed King of Leinster. This was the beginning of the long process of colonisation that would dictate the terms of Ireland's development over the next seven hundred years. The Anglo-Normans replaced the Viking town of Dublin with a medieval walled city and the wooden structures of Christ Church and St Patrick's cathedrals were rebuilt in stone. To prevent the Anglo-Normans growing too independent of the English crown, Henry II established a court in Dublin and the city became the centre of his power in Ireland.

By the 18th century the city was booming. The estates of the Anglo-Normans and later English settlers, descendants of the adventurers who had been rewarded by the English crown with land confiscated from rebel Gaelic chieftains or disloyal Anglo-Normans, were bringing in handsome profits. A period of relative stability and, consequently, prosperity set in. The legacy of this Georgian heyday is clearly visible all around Dublin. Some of the greatest architects of the time replanned the city, imposing a formal order on the existing muddle with confident wide streets, gracious townhouses and generous squares. Skilled stonemasons, stuccodores and craftsmen came from Europe to decorate these ornate townhouses.

After 1800 and the Act of Union, which dissolved the Irish parliament, Dublin fell on hard times. Many of the Protestant Anglo-Irish ruling class left for London, becoming absentee landlords. The Georgian splendour they left behind decayed into tenement squalor. Victorian civic spiritedness contributed some new public buildings of note, but it fell to philanthropic business folk such as the Guinness family to restore and maintain the earlier architectural gems. The fight for independence and a Civil War in 1922 took their toll on Dublin's streets, and many important buildings were scarred by fighting. Since then neglect and lack of vision has been responsible for the loss of many fine buildings, the wonderful vista up Winetavern Street to the 12th century Christ Church cathedral, for example, has been obscured by the massive drums of the Civic Office buildings, nicknamed 'the Bunkers'. In the late 1980s a new awareness of the city's architectural strengths appeared alongside a period of economic growth, and an effort to restore rather than demolish Dublin's Georgian heritage has since been made. The warren of warehouses and narrow 18th century alleys of Temple Bar, for example, has become a showpiece of restoration and experimental modern architecture. The Dublin Bay that attracted successive waves of invaders is difficult to discern now under the commercial and residential sprawl of Dublin and its suburbs which sustain a population of over one million people. Dublin city is changing fast and the speed of that change is partly fuelled by its youthful population – over 50 percent are under the age of twenty-five and that makes the city come alive. Today Dublin is a city full of charm with a vigorous cultural life, small enough to be friendly, yet cosmopolitan in outlook.

SOUTHEAST DUBLIN

Trinity College

Trinity College is the oldest university in the country and was founded in 1592 by Queen Elizabeth I of England on the confiscated grounds of the former Priory of All Hallows. Up until then the Protestant Anglo-Irish ruling class had been sending their sons to the Continent to be educated where they ran the risk of becoming 'infected with Popery'. Trinity was to become the centre of Protestant education and for 250 years was the only university in Ireland. It continued to be used mainly by the Protestant population until the second half of this century – until 1966 Catholics who studied at Trinity had to obtain a special dispensation from their archbishop or risk excommunication. By 1990, however, roughly 75 per cent of the 8,000 students at Trinity were Catholic.

The college sits at the heart of Dublin. Its 90m curved facade ends a long vista down Dame Street, one of the city's main thoroughfares. While none of the original 16th century buildings now survives, the campus provides a fascinating guide to the work of many important architects over the centuries. The restrained facade, which acts as a balance to the exuberance of the Bank of Ireland building opposite, was designed by Theodore Jacobsen in the mid-18th century. Behind its facade lie a number of interconnecting cobbled quadrangles surrounded by mainly 18th century buildings with some Victorian and 20th century additions.

The first and largest of the quadrangles is **Front Square** or **Parliament Square** (the building costs were met by Parliament). On either side of Front Square two wings of student residences ensure that Trinity plays a lively part in Dublin social and cultural life. Beyond the residences and set back a little from Front Square are two matched porticos – on the right the **Exam Hall** and on the left the **Chapel**, with splendid plasterwork by Michael Stapleton – both designed in the classical style by the Scottish architect Sir William Chambers. They were built in the 1780s, and are the last Georgian additions to the college. Beside the Chapel stands the **Dining Hall**, designed in the 1740s by the German architect Richard Cassells who is responsible for much of Georgian Dublin. Destroyed by fire in 1984, it has since been beautifully refurbished and the adjoining building, the **Atrium,** has been hollowed out to form a three storey-high performance space, which is overlooked by wooden galleries.

Top, *Trinity College is the oldest university in Ireland, established in 1592 by Queen Elizabeth I, bottom, left, the grounds are full of sculpture, both modern such as 'Sphere with Sphere', by Arnaldo Pomodoro, and classical.*

Left, *the campanile is believed to mark the spot of the high altar of All Hallows' Priory which once stood on these grounds,* right, *the former Provost George Salmon by sculptor John Hughes.*

In the centre of Front Square the Victorian baroque **campanile**, donated by the Archbishop of Armagh in 1853, is believed to stand on the spot once occupied by the high altar of the Priory of All Hallows. During students' ragweek, the campanile is often decorated with bicycles and other unexpected ornaments.

The **Rubrics**, the red-brick student residences which stand directly behind the campanile, are the oldest set of buildings in the college, dating back to 1701 and the reign of Queen Anne, but even these were revamped in the Victorian period. Richard Cassells also contributed the **Printing House**, a miniature Doric temple and an architectural gem, which stands in **New Square** behind the Rubrics. Completed in 1734, it was his earliest Dublin work. Another building worth noting in the same square is the **Museum Building**, designed in the Venetian Gothic style in 1852 by Sir Thomas Deane and Benjamin Woodward. It was to influence the work of architects for the remainder of the century. Outside, are wonderful stone carvings of animals, fruit and flowers, while the grand marble interior is home to a skeleton of the giant Irish Elk. Deane and Woodward also enlarged **Trinity Library**, designed by Thomas Burgh in 1792.

Modern buildings such as the **Arts Block**, a tiered concrete library and lecture hall complex, and the **Berkeley Library**, with its massive concrete and granite facade, both designed by Ahrends, Burton and Koralek, were added in the 1970s and 1980s and enclose the remaining sides of the square formed by Burgh's Library. Overlooking the **Sports Field**, the new Samuel Beckett Theatre Centre, a tall wooden structure on stilts, designed by Dublin architects de Blacam and Meagher in the early 1990s, houses two theatres for student and experimental work.

Many interesting sculptural works, both modern and classical, populate the campus. Those outside the front of Trinity commemorate two well-known *alumni*, philosopher and orator Edmund Burke (1729-97) and Oliver Goldsmith (1728-74), author of *She Stoops to Conquer* and *The Vicar of Wakefield*. Many other noted Anglo-Irish figures studied at Trinity including the satirist Jonathan Swift (1667-1745), patriot Wolfe Tone (1763-98), Oscar Wilde (1854-1900), JM Synge (1871-1909) whose *Playboy of the Western World* caused riots when first shown at the Abbey Theatre, and Nobel Prizewinner Samuel Beckett (1906-91).

Top, *the Long Room of Trinity College Library contains the 8th century illuminated manuscript known as* The Book of Kells, *bottom, left, a bust of the satirist Dean Jonathan Swift, who was a student at Trinity College.*

Trinity Library

Designed in 1792 by Thomas Burgh, **Trinity Library** contains the famous **Long Room** which at 64 metres by 12.2 metres is the largest single chamber library in Europe. In 1859, Sir Thomas Deane and Benjamin Woodward added a barrel-vaulted ceiling, which gives the library both much needed extra space and a lofty elegance.

Best known of the library's treasures is *The Book of Kells*, an 8th century manuscript of the four gospels produced either in the *scriptorium* of the monastery at Kells in County Meath or on Iona off the coast of Scotland. Many Irish monasteries had *scriptoria* attached where scribes laboured over pre-Christian legends, epics and histories as well as the scriptures. In the margins they often jotted down poems of praise or complaint – some of them very witty. It is thanks to these scribes – and the missionaries who went to the Continent during the Dark Ages – that Ireland earned itself the name of the 'Land of Saints and Scholars'. These illuminated manuscripts were highly prized and so always under threat of theft – a few pages at the front and back of *The Book of Kells* have been lost, perhaps when the book was stolen from Kells in 1006 and stripped of its gold cover.

Top, *views of the rotunda of the National Library on Kildare Street from outside and,* bottom, right, *from within.*

The National Library

The **National Library** on Kildare Street was once the library of the Royal Dublin Society (RDS), an institution committed to promoting advances in science, agriculture and the arts. Together with the **National Museum**, which faces it across the lawn of **Leinster House**, the two seats of education were envisaged as providing a cultural centre for Dubliners. The library building was designed by Sir Thomas Deane in 1890. Thousands of books, magazines, newspapers, maps and manuscripts relating to Ireland, including those collected by the RDS, are lodged here. The library also has a significant collection of first editions and preserves the manuscripts of leading Irish authors, complete with revisions, margin notes and doodles. The circular **Reading Room** is a delight to work in – as many of Ireland's finest modern writers have discovered. In fact, James Joyce, who frequented the library himself, sited the great literary debate in *Ulysses* here.

Top left, *the National Gallery of Ireland*, top, right, *Victorian cast-iron work hides the fact that the Mansion House dates from 1710*, bottom, left, *Leinster House, seat of government.*

National Gallery

Playwright George Bernard Shaw (1856-1950) claimed that his whole life was influenced by the **National Gallery** 'for I spent many days of my boyhood wandering through it and so learned to care for art'. In gratitude he bequeathed one-third of his royalties to the gallery and as a result enabled substantial purchases to be made. The gallery is composed of three sections – the Dargan Wing houses European art from the Renaissance onwards with a recently discovered Caravaggio, some good Rembrandts, Titians and Tintorettos; the Modern Wing is devoted to 20th century European art especially that of the Impressionists; the Milltown Rooms contain Irish art – mainly Anglo-Irish works from the 17th century on, with an entire room devoted to Jack B Yeats (1871-1957), brother of poet William Butler Yeats.

Mansion House

Home to Dublin's lord mayors since 1715. Although the exterior has been reworked with Victorian details, the house is one of the oldest in the area, dating from 1710. The interior still shows its Queen Anne origins.

Top, *buskers on Grafton Street, one of Dublin's busiest shopping streets,* bottom, right, *shoppers relax outside a famous Victorian pub.*

Leinster House

The seat of Ireland's parliament, or *Dáil Éireann*, is **Leinster House**, built in 1745 for the Earl of Kildare in the days when fashionable folk lived on the north side of the Liffey. 'Wherever I go,' the Earl is supposed to have said, 'they will follow.' And he was right, the green fields which surrounded him were quickly developed into **Merrion Square**. The Royal Dublin Society owned Leinster House from 1814 until the Irish government purchased it in 1925.

Grafton Street

Dublin's smartest shopping street bustles with shoppers, jewellery makers, buskers and flower sellers. The many Victorian pubs, such as McDaids, in the sidestreets, offer a chance to sit and watch the crowds go by.

St Stephen's Green

Until the philanthropist Lord Ardilaun, Sir Arthur Guinness, tidied up **St Stephen's Green** in 1880 and gave it to the public, the park had been leased to the house-owners around the square.

Sadly, most of these original houses fell victim to building developers in the 1960s, but the survivors are fine examples of the best townhouses of Georgian Dublin. On the south side at Nos 85-86 is **Newman House**, beautifully restored to its 18th century splendour. No 85 was designed by Richard Cassells in 1738 and contains unique plasterwork executed by the famous Italian stuccodores, the Francini brothers. In the 19th century, Newman House became the home of University College Dublin (UCD), the Catholic alternative to Trinity College, where the English poet Gerard Manley Hopkins lectured until he died of typhoid in 1889. Shortly after Hopkins's death James Joyce became a student here – and he immortalised the experience in *A Portrait of the Artist as a Young Man*. In the 1960s UCD moved out to the suburbs at the instigation of the Catholic Archbishop of Dublin who feared that students might be contaminated by their proximity to the Protestant college of Trinity. Beside No 85 is **University Church**, its plain exterior hiding a Byzantine fantasy inside. On the north side of the square, the gentlemen's clubs which lead up to the **Shelbourne Hotel** are a reminder of the days when St Stephen's Green was an exclusive address.

Just as Lord Ardilaun intended, St Stephen's Green has become a popular park and Dubliners love to sunbathe, picnic or feed the ducks and swans who flock here. Dotted all around the park are bandstands, benches, formal flowerbeds, statues – Joyce stands opposite his old college – and ornamental lakes. There is also a garden for the blind with scented plants labelled in braille.

Clockwise from top, Dubliners love to picnic in St Stephen's Green; a bust of James Joyce faces his old college; dotted around the park are benches and bandstands, fountains and flowerbeds; the Fusiliers Arch entrance to the park.

Merrion Square

Dublin is famous for its Georgian streetscapes and one of the best preserved is **Merrion Square** which was built in the 1760s for Lord Fitzwilliam. Overall, Georgian houses may appear uniform, but each differs in its details – the doors and heavy brass doorknockers, delicate fanlights, cast-iron footscrapers and balconies. Many of the houses have plaques commemorating famous inhabitants – **No 1** was the childhood home of Oscar Wilde, while politician Daniel O'Connell, who campaigned for and won Catholic Emancipation in 1829, lived at **No 50**. Today, most of the houses are offices, but the square comes alive at weekends when amateur painters hang their work on the park railings.

Fitzwilliam Street

Fitzwilliam Street, which runs from **Leeson Street** down to **Holles Street Hospital**, incorporating **Fitzwilliam Place** and the east side of **Merrion Square**, was once Europe's longest Georgian street. In the 1960s, however, a group of houses was demolished to make way for the modern office block which now interrrupts the vista.

Top and middle, *elaborate doorways and details from Georgian houses in Merrion Square*, bottom, right, *Fitzwilliam Street, once the longest Georgian Street in Europe.*

SOUTHWEST DUBLIN

Dublin Castle

Dublin Castle comes as a surprise – it no longer looks like a castle (only the **Record Tower** survives from its days as a fortified structure, and even its castellations are 19th century additions). It is a hotch-potch of architectural styles, part modern, part medieval, but most of its buildings date from the elegant Dublin of the 18th century, and are grouped around an **Upper** and **Lower Yard**. For over 700 years there was no greater symbol of British power in Ireland than 'the Castle' and virtually every rebellion against the English aimed to overthrow it. None succeeded.

Built in 1204 on high ground to the south of the Liffey, the castle was originally bound on three sides by the Poddle river. Just below the castle walls the Poddle ran into a pool, the Black Pool or 'Dubh Linn' after which the city is named. Remains of a Viking fort, circa 9th century, found during excavations in 1990, indicate that the site had always been of strategic importance and it is believed that an earlier rath existed here.

Originally, a sturdy tower guarded each corner of the curtain walls around a quadrangle roughly corresponding to the present Upper Yard, while the portcullis was at the centre of the **North Gate**. By 1242 a chapel had been built and fitted with stained glass windows. A spacious hall where **St Patrick's Hall** now stands had been built and rebuilt by 1320. This original castle must have inspired respect – not only were rebels regularly decapitated and their heads used to decorate the castle walls, but there was the unique luxury of piped water.

For the first few centuries of British rule the castle was a constant target of attack during Irish rebellions. Silken Thomas, son of the Earl of Kildare, besieged the castle with cannons in 1534. Unfortunately for him, the city's officials were sitting inside the impregnable walls with large stocks of food and gunpowder. Not only was Silken Thomas captured, but he and five of his uncles were hung.

In 1684 a fire devastated the residential quarters of the castle. They were rebuilt with a greater awareness of the castle's administrative functions – additional reception rooms and offices were included and the **Upper** and **Lower Yards** became recognisable in their present form.

Dublin Castle is a mix of architectural periods, top, left, the Record Tower, dating from 1207, with on one side 18th century buildings and on the other the Gothic Revival chapel by Francis Johnston, bottom, left, the Upper Yard, showing Bedford Tower which encloses the old west tower of the gate-house. It was from here that the Irish crown jewels were stolen in 1907 – and never seen again.

But the castle still acted as the military centre and prison for the city. For three years, 15 year old Hugh Roe O'Donnell was held hostage in the **Record Tower** to ensure the good behaviour of his Ulster clan – a common English practice. On Christmas Eve 1592, he and some companions escaped, dressed only in fine linens and sandals. It was a freezing night with blizzards and howling gales and their journey took them on foot over the Wicklow mountains to Glenmalure. Hugh Roe survived to be extolled by Irish *fíle* or bards, but his companions died of exposure.

Rebuilding continued throughout the 18th century as the castle's role again altered. As the residence of the Viceroy, the representative of English power in Ireland, it became the epicentre of Anglo-Irish society, hosting balls and levées and entertaining visiting dignatories. Sir William Robinson who had designed the Royal Hospital Kilmainham carried out much of the work, while Sir Edward Lovett Pearce redecorated **St Patrick's Hall**. Much of the Georgian **Upper Yard** with the **Castle Hall**, simple and elegant in red brick, dates from this period, and for the hundred years from the end of the 18th century onwards, additions, reconstructions and amendments were constant.

In 1798 the British quashed another rebellion. It was a particularly bloody episode, with rebel corpses being laid out in the castle yard as trophies. One corpse was seen to move and, after being resuscitated, was granted a pardon but, as one observer commented, the rebel 'did not, however, change his principles'.

By 1814 the **Chapel Royal**, now called the **Church of the Most Holy Trinity**, adjoining the **Record Tower,** had been designed in the Gothic Revival style by Francis Johnston. Inside are the coat of arms of every viceroy since the 12th century, with elaborate fan vaulting and plasterwork by stuccodore Michael Stapleton. Outside, Edward Smyth, known for his work on the Custom House and Four Courts, carved over a hundred stone heads of mythological and historical figures. The chapel was immediately proclaimed 'the most beautiful specimen of the Gothic style of Architecture in Europe'.

During the Rising of 1916, the castle was attacked once more, again without success. The castle was finally handed over to the Irish State in 1922 and now houses government offices, as well as the manuscripts and treasures of the **Chester Beatty Library and Gallery of Oriental Art** and, in the Record Tower, the **Garda Museum**. One function of the castle has not changed, however, it is still used to entertain visiting dignatories.

Top, right, interior of the Church of the Most Holy Trinity with exuberant plasterwork by Michael Stapleton, bottom, right, 18th century painted panels in the ceiling of St Patrick's Hall, bottom, left, an ornate mirror in the Picture Gallery.

City Hall

Gazing down **Parliament Street** and across the **Liffey** to **Capel Street** is **City Hall**, once the Royal Exchange. Built in 1769 by the Dublin Guild of Merchants, it was turned over to government forces during the 1798 Rebellion for use as an interrogation and torture chamber. Nowadays it houses the offices of Dublin Corporation.

College Green and Dame Street

Dame Street leads from **College Green**, just outside the front gates of **Trinity College**, to **City Hall** and on to **Lord Edward Street** and **Christ Church Cathedral**. Outside City Hall it passes the site of Dame Gate, the entrance through the city walls to the medieval town. In the early 18th century, Dame Street was the main street outside the walls of the city and connected the vital centres of power, **Dublin Castle,** which stands behind City Hall, and the **House of Parliament,** now the headquarters of the Bank of Ireland opposite **Trinity College**.

The street also contains many buildings in the style known as 'bankers' Georgian' as well as the modern **Central Bank**.

Top, left, City Hall faces down Parliament Street towards the River Liffey, bottom, a view up Dame Street from Trinity College.

Christ Church Cathedral

Christ Church Cathedral stands within the original medieval city walls. Dublin's oldest cathedral, it was founded in 1037 by Sitric Silkenbeard, the king of Viking Dublin. A convert to Christianity he made two pilgrimages to Rome and died, like his father, a monk on the island of Iona off the coast of Scotland. The structure that Silkenbeard had built was made of wood, but over the period 1173 and 1240 the Anglo-Normans rebuilt Silkenbeard's church in stone. This seventy-year long construction period meant that the style of the cathedral encompasses two architectural periods: parts, such as the nave, were built in the Gothic style, while others, among them the **choir** and **transepts**, were built in the Romanesque. A small elongated **head** over the Romanesque doorway in the **south transept** may commemorate either King Henry II of England or Dermot MacMurrough, the King of Leinster responsible for inviting Strongbow, the Earl of Pembroke, and his force of Anglo-Normans into Ireland and thus beginning the long process of colonisation.

By the 19th century the cathedral was in tatters. The whiskey distiller Henry Roe funded a total restoration in 1871 – a mixed blessing as most of the original building was lost and the 14th century choir was demolished and replaced in mock Romanesque style.

Apart from the medieval **crypt,** Dublin's oldest building, where some of the richly carved stone capitals are preserved, the **transepts** and the north elevation of the **nave**, little of the 13th century structure remains. The **crypt** is full of macabre relics. The heart of **St Lawrence O'Toole**, the Archbishop of Dublin during the time of Strongbow's invasion, lies in a heart-shaped metal box in **St Laud's chapel**. Strongbow himself is also supposed to be buried here. But it is likely that his tomb was destroyed in a roof-fall and replaced by the effigy of another knight. Legend has it that the smaller of two effigies in the crypt contains the body of his son which was cut in two for cowardice in battle, it is more likely to contain Strongbow's intestines. The gruesome remains of a mummified rat and cat, caught in a chase behind the organ pipes, are displayed in a glass case. An ancient tunnel is believed to lead from the crypt and under the Liffey to what is now the Four Courts. According to legend, a soldier attending a state funeral in Christ Church in the Middle

Top, *Christ Church Cathedral, founded by the Vikings in 1037 and rebuilt by the Anglo-Normans.*

Top, left, the Romanesque doorway of Christ Church Cathedral, top, right, *the interior of the cathedral was restored in 1871,* bottom, left, *St Audoen's Church and 17th century bell tower.*

Ages, wandered down the tunnel to relieve his boredom. The sacristan unwittingly locked the soldier into the tunnel and his gnawed body was found several months later, sword in hand. Around him lay the corpses of over 200 rats he had slaughtered!

St Audoen's Church

Built in 1190 on the remains of an early Christian site dedicated to St Columcille, and named after the Norman St Ouen of Rouen, **St Audoen's** on High Street is the oldest medieval parish church surviving in Dublin. However, the only reminder of its early Christian roots is the gravestone inside the porch known as the '**lucky stone**', which is said to bring good fortune to anyone who touches it. The **west doorway** of the original building still survives, while the **bell tower** contains a peal of bells dating from 1423 and said to be the oldest in Ireland. These bells were rung during storms to remind Dubliners to pray for those at sea. The churchyard is bound by a restored section of the old **city walls**, with steps leading down to **St Audoen's Arch**, the only gateway to the old city still standing.

Top, *St Patrick's Park and Cathedral,* bottom, right, *the interior was completely refurbished in 1864.*

St Patrick's Cathedral

Dublin's second Protestant cathedral stands on the oldest Christian site in Dublin, and one believed to be connected with Ireland's patron saint, St Patrick. It suffered a similar history to that of its neighbour Christ Church Cathedral – rebuilt in 1190 in stone in the 'early English' style, it too fell into decay over the centuries. It was also thoroughly restored in 1864 with funds from another drinks merchant, Sir Benjamin Lee Guinness, whose **statue** stands to the right of the entrance. Unlike Christ Church, however, St Patrick's Cathedral stood outside the medieval city walls in the area known as '**the Liberties**' and so became the people's cathedral rather than the place where ceremonies of state were performed.

Perhaps the best-known figure associated with St Patrick's is Jonathan Swift, author *of Gulliver's Travels* and many other satires, and dean at the cathedral from 1713-1745. Hugely generous, Swift gave away half his income every year and on his death, the local citizenry pleaded for so many locks of his hair as mementoes that he was buried bald. He is buried in the cathedral beside his beloved Esther Johnson.

Brazen Head Pub

Established in 1198, the **Brazen Head** on **Lower Bridge Street** is the oldest pub in Dublin. It has a venerable history – it was also the place where the rebels of the United Irishmen rising of 1798 used to meet to plan their campaign. Nowadays, it plays host to traditional music sessions every night of the week.

Temple Bar

The narrow cobbled streets of Temple Bar are so full of charm that it is hard to believe that until recently the area was under threat of demolition. Once filled with rundown artists' studios, secondhand clothes shops, printers' warehouses and musty pubs, Temple Bar is now the pride of Dublin Corporation with expensive apartments, art galleries, restaurants, nightclubs and the art deco Clarence Hotel owned – and frequented – by U2. But most of all there are its pubs … The pub is central to Irish social life and the best command fierce loyalty and are known far and wide for serving a 'good pint' – a 'pint' always means Guinness. Pulling a *good* pint is an art – and the test of a skilled barman – it takes time and patience and the end result should taste as smooth as velvet.

Top, left, The Brazen Head is Dublin's oldest pub, during summer its courtyard is packed with locals and tourists, while inside, bottom, traditional musicians offer entertainment every night.

Top, the evidence of a busy night –
empty beer kegs outside the Oliver
St John Gogarty Pub in Temple
Bar, middle, drinking graffiti,
bottom, left and right,
the exterior and interior of
a fine Victorian pub on
Fleet Street in Temple Bar.

Guinness Storehouse

Emigrants sigh for it, songs extol its virtues, nursing mothers were encouraged to drink it. Guinness is Ireland's national drink and the brewery set up in 1759 by Arthur Guinness (*bottom right*), now fills over four million pints a day and is enshrined in Dublin's architec-tural history – the philanthropic Guinness family restored **St Patrick's Cathedral**, donated **St Stephen's Green** to the public, cleared slums and replaced them with the **Iveagh Trust** buildings, swimming baths and hostel on Patrick Street.

A visit to the home of Guinness is a high point of any visit to Dublin. The exciting state-of-the-art exhibition, housed in the pint-shaped Guinness Storehouse, explains all about this famous beer. Relax with your pint in the seventh-floor Gravity Bar and enjoy the incredible 360° view of Dublin.

Royal Hospital Kilmainham

Now the **Irish Museum of Modern Art**, the **Royal Hospital Kilmainham** was built in 1680 to house old soldiers and continued to do so until 1922. Inspired by Les Invalides in Paris it was designed by the General Surveyor Sir William Robinson under the direction of the viceroy, the Duke of Ormond. The design is simple and restrained – a colonnaded building with a spire on one side, constructed around a central courtyard. The **hall** and **chapel** interiors are unique – the chapel ceiling is ornamented with relief work of floral and fruit motifs. The hall now hosts classical concerts, while the rest of the museum houses changing collections of Irish and European modern art.

Kilmainham Gaol

Built in 1788 in time to house the rebel leaders of the doomed 1798 revolt, this grim prison also held the leaders of the 1916 Rising. The British decided to execute fifteen of the leaders over a number of days. One, James Connolly was so badly wounded that he had to be tied to a chair to face the firing squad. It was one of the worst calculated moves the British had ever made in Ireland and transformed the Rising from a military failure into a romantic gesture that inspired the nationalist cause.

Marsh's Library

The first public library in Ireland was designed in 1701 by Sir William Robinson to house the library of Archbishop Narcissus Marsh. Virtually unchanged since, the library is divided into reading cubicles by Gothic screens which bear the Archbishop's coat of arms. Readers were once kept in the cubicles under lock and key to safeguard the more valuable manuscripts. Over 25,000 books dating from the 16th century onwards are still housed here.

Top, right, *the former hospital at Kilmainham is now a museum of modern art*, middle, *Kilmainham Gaol where patriots were imprisoned*, bottom, *Marsh's Library dates from 1701.*

NORTH OF THE LIFFEY

The Liffey

It is because of the River Liffey and its many tributaries that Dublin has more than one name. In Irish it is *Baile Atha Cliath* or 'Town at the Ford of the Hurdles' – the ford dated from before the Vikings and resembled a causeway that spanned the river, which in those days was very wide and shallow. Then there is the city's English name, *Dubh Linn* or 'Black Pool', named after the pool of water formed by the Poddle river as it joined the Liffey near Dublin Castle. To complicate matters further, the section of Liffey passing through the city also had a name – *Ruirthech* or 'Turbulent River'. Just how turbulent it was can be judged from an entry in the ancient *Annals* which records that in 770AD an entire Ulster army drowned as it attempted to wade across.

Now, the Liffey is better behaved and, constrained between the quays, it runs quietly out into the sea at Ringsend, dividing Dublin neatly into two – the southside with its chic shopping streets, expensive restaurants, pubs and nightclubs and the northside where James Gandon's splendid public buildings are surrounded by delapidated Georgian squares.

O'Connell Bridge

Designed by James Gandon in 1790 to link the south side of Dublin to the north, the bridge is roughly as broad as it is long and continues north up **O'Connell Street**, Dublin's main thoroughfare.

General Post Office

The **General Post Office** (GPO) is the most significant building on **O'Connell Street**, not so much for its architectural merit as for its place in Irish history. On Easter Monday 1916 a small band of rebels made it their headquarters and their poet leader, Pádraig Pearse, stood outside to read the Proclamation of the Irish Republic to the few disinterested passersby. A week of shelling by British troops followed, leaving the GPO and most of **Lower O'Connell Street** gutted. The rebels evacuated to **Moore Street** and surrendered soon after. It was a disastrous military defeat. But from then on, Irish independence became just a matter of time. In the Civil War of 1922 O'Connell Street again suffered and only the facade of the GPO remained. Now beautifully restored and a working post office it houses a statue of '*The Fall of Cúchulainn*', the mythic Ulster hero, to commemorate the 1916 Rising.

Facing page, top, O'Connell Bridge with the dome of Gandon's famous Custom House outlined against the Financial Centre, bottom left, the view south from O'Connell Bridge, bottom right, the Spire, O'Connell Street.

This page top, the Lír clock, a Dublin landmark, bottom, right, the GPO.

Custom House

In 1779 architect James Gandon turned down an offer to work in St Petersburg. Instead he came to Dublin to work on what would become one of the finest examples of Georgian building in Britain. Gandon remained in Ireland for the rest of his life, contributing two more splendid public buildings to Dublin's architecture – the **Four Courts** and **King's Inns**.

Begun in 1781 and costing £400,000 over ten years, the Custom House was not an easy project – the site was sea-sodden and required constant draining and elaborate foundations to prevent subsidence, workmen demanded constant wage increases, the enemies of the project hired mobs to vandalise the construction and Gandon found it wise to wear his sword whenever he visited. But none of these obstacles nor a fire nor even the death of his wife deterred Gandon, and in 1791 the Custom House, built of gleaming Portland stone, was finished.

The **south front** with its graceful Corinthian portico flanked by arcades faces onto the river, while the **north front** faces onto what remains of the Georgian Gardiner Street. The fourteen **Riverine Heads** over the doors and windows, depicting the main rivers of Ireland, and the figure of **Commerce** on the dome are by the sculptor Edward Smyth, Gandon's discovery who, he declared, was the equal of Michelangelo.

In 1921 the Custom House was targeted by nationalist forces. A fire raged for days melting down brass fittings and causing cracks in the stonework. Restored in 1926, the drum of the dome was replaced by Irish Ardbraccan stone rather than the white Portland stone of the original and it has aged badly. By the 1970s more major renovations were necessary and the present Custom House was unveiled in 1991.

Top, left, *the south front of the Custom House built by James Gandon,* bottom, left, *behind the recently built International Financial Services Centre.*

Top, *the Four Courts by James Gandon is a masterpiece
of Georgian Dublin,* bottom, right, *St Michan's Church founded in
1096 by the Vikings.*

Four Courts

The second of James Gandon's landmark Georgian
buildings, the **Four Courts** was commissioned by the
Duke of Rutland in 1796 to replace the decaying
courts near Christ Church. It contains several Gandon
flourishes – facing onto the river with a central
Corinthian portico and side wings connected by arcades, with sculptural work by Edward Smyth.

St Michan's Church

Only the tower now survives of the church founded
by the Vikings in 1096 and for centuries the only
parish church north of the Liffey. The interior is plain
but contains an organ on which Handel is believed to
have played while composing 'The Messiah'. But St
Michan's is best known for the mummified bodies
that are preserved in its 17th century vaults. Outside in
the graveyard, drawn perhaps by the macabre
corpses in the vaults, Bram Stoker, the author of
Dracula, used to pace.

Around O'Connell Street

Henry Moore, Earl of Drogheda, originally planned the area around O'Connell Street. His desire for immortality led him to commemorate his entire title in their names – **Henry Street**, **Moore Street, Earl Street**, **Of Lane** and **Drogheda Street** (now the top of O'Connell Street). Henry and Moore streets are busy shopping areas, with department stores and shopping centres offering the best bargains in town. Moore Street is famous for the ranks of street-traders advertising their wares in singsong Dublin accents.

Facing page, top, right, the Hugh Lane Municipal Gallery of Modern Art on Parnell Square, bottom, in the Dublin Writers' Museum, built in the heyday of Georgian Dublin, the elegant Gallery of Writers is decorated with elaborate stucco work.

This page, an exile for most of his adult life, James Joyce set all of his works in a minutely described Dublin. In fact, he claimed that if Dublin was ever destroyed it could be rebuilt brick by brick from the descriptions in his writings. Top, left, his statue stands in North Earl Street, bottom, left, Henry Street thronged with bargain hunters, bottom, middle and right, and Moore Street traders.

Hugh Lane
Municipal Gallery of Modern Art

This art museum was once the townhouse of the Earl of Charlemont, appropriately enough a patron of the arts. It was designed by Sir William Chambers in 1762 in the days when the rich and powerful lived north of the Liffey and is one of the pleasantest galleries in Dublin to browse in because of its compact size. Its collection of 19th and 20th century European art includes Impressionist works collected by Sir Hugh Lane, an art dealer who bequeathed his collection to Dublin Corporation in 1908. After his death aboard the torpedoed *Lusitania* in 1915, a legal battle raged between Dublin and London as to who should own the collection. It has only recently been resolved and the pictures are now shared by the Tate Gallery in London and the Hugh Lane.

Dublin Writers' Museum

Two doors away from the Gallery, at **Nos 18** and **19 Parnell Square**, are the **Dublin Writers' Museum** and **Irish Writers' Centre** respectively. Ireland is known for its writers – four have received the Nobel Prize for Literature, William Butler Yeats, George Bernard Shaw, Samuel Beckett and Seamus Heaney, and their work and lives, and that of many other famous writers, are covered here.

Parnell Square

Construction began on **Parnell Square** in the 1750s. By the 1780s it boasted more peers, politicians and bishops among its residents than any other street in Dublin. The square was originally named Rutland Square after the viceroy of the period, but it was later renamed in memory of the nationalist leader, Charles Stewart Parnell, whose statue stands at the top of O'Connell Street. The centre of the square used to contain the Pleasure Gardens, a fundraising venture in the 1740s by Dr Bartholomew Mosse, the barber-surgeon who used the entrance fees from patrons to finance the building of the Lying-in (Rotunda) Hospital on the south side of Parnell Square. It was the first maternity hospital in Europe and is still in use. All that now remains of the Gardens is a small square of green on the north side of Parnell Square, opposite the **Dublin Writers' Museum**, called the **Garden of Remembrance** which commemorates the 1916 Rising.

King's Inns

Designed in 1786, the **King's Inns** was the last of James Gandon's great public buildings and still serves its original function of providing training and facilities for barristers. While the foundation stone was laid by the Earl of Clare in 1795, construction did not begin until 1802. Gandon had left Ireland in 1797, suspecting rightly that the city was on the point of revolution. When he returned after the 1798 rebellion he faced a backlog of work. He was nearly sixty years of age by this time and suffering acutely from gout and so he passed the bulk of the work on the King's Inns to his protegée Henry Aaron Baker. The building was finally

completed in 1817, by which time Gandon had long since retired to his house in north Dublin.

Like the Four Courts and the Custom House the King's Inns was designed to front onto water – a branch of the Royal Canal once extended past here. A graceful **cupola** rises over the central archway. On the left a doorway leads to the diningroom – Irish barristers must consume a set number of dinners per year. On either side of the doorway are two female **caryatides** by Edward Smyth, the sculptor favoured by James Gandon. On the left is Cares, goddess of food, while on the right stands a follower of Bacchus holding a wine goblet. The figures flanking the doorway to the right of the central archway are more sober. This is the doorway to the former prerogative court, now the Registry of Deeds, and the figures represent 'Law', carrying a book and a quill, and 'Security' with a key and scroll.

Top, *the gracious facade of King's Inns, James Gandon's last public building,* top, right, *the stonework is by Edward Smyth who worked with Gandon on most of his projects,* middle, *the figure of 'Security' holds a key and a scroll,* bottom, *two male caryatides flanking the doorway to the Registry of Deeds.*

Phoenix Park

Named not for the mythical bird but from a corruption of the Irish *fionn uisce* or 'clear water', the **Phoenix Park** was formed in 1662 when 2,000 acres of land surrounding the Viceregal residence, known as Phoenix Manor, were turned into a royal deer park. Lord Chesterfield opened the park to the public in 1747 when shrubs and paths were laid out in much their present form. The Park contains many monuments, as well as **Dublin Zoo**, famous for its success in breeding lions, its best-known offspring is the roaring lion on the MGM film logo.

Garden of Remembrance, Islandbridge

Nearly 150,000 Irishmen fought in the First World War, and the 50,000 who died are commemorated in the **Garden of Remembrance at Islandbridge**. Sir Edward Lutyens designed the memorial, which stands on 20 acres and is overlooked by **Magazine Hill** in Phoenix Park. Work was carried out by hand to give maximum employment to the workforce of ex-soldiers.

Top, middle, and bottom, left, *peaceful scenes from Phoenix Park,* bottom, right, *Memorial Park, zoological garden.*

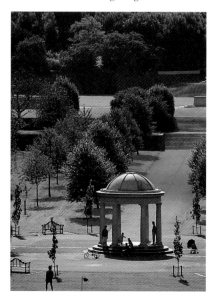

Top, *a quiet stretch of the Grand Canal,* bottom, right, *Portobello House, built by the Grand Canal Company in 1807 as one of five hotels on the route between Dublin and the Shannon, had a varied life. When passenger boats no longer used the canal it became a home for blind women and later a nursing home (the artist Jack B Yeats spent his last years there), until finally it became Portobello College.*

Grand Canal

In 1715 an act of parliament proposed a canal link between Dublin and the rivers Shannon in the west and Barrow in the south. As a result two canals were built – the **Royal Canal** on the northside of Dublin, and the **Grand Canal** which met the Liffey at Ringsend, cut south of the city past **Portobello** and **Dolphin's Barn** where there was a harbour, and led eventually to the Shannon. However, once the railways were firmly established these waterways were no longer competitive, and commercial traffic stopped in the 1960s. Since then the canals have been left to those who enjoy walking along its grassy towpath.

AROUND DUBLIN

Dublin sits in a magnificent bay which stretches south to Killiney and north to the tiny fishing port of Howth. Bronze Age sites, historic castles and abbeys and sublime views as well as associations with famous writers, poets and painters make the Dublin coastline one well worth exploring.

South of Dublin, the Victorian seaside town of **Dun Laoghaire** is the yachting centre of the east coast. It has four yachtclubs and a fine harbour bound by two mile-long stone piers which point out into Dublin Bay. In the long summer evenings the piers are thronged with Dubliners watching the racing yachts vie for space around the race marks.

A mile or so south of **Dun Laoghaire** in **Sandycove**, a **Martello Tower** stands on the edge of the shoreline, one of a string of twenty-five coastal defensive structures built in anticipation of an invasion by Napoleon. None of them ever saw action and they have been converted into shops, homes, museums or left to crumble. The Sandycove tower now houses memorabilia of Ireland's most famous exile, James Joyce, who once spent a few days here. His friend, the Dublin surgeon, writer and wit Oliver St John Gogarty, sometimes stayed in the tower to write his poetry. In 1904, Joyce joined him. A few days later, however, they quarreled and Joyce moved out. Gogarty said he would have thrown him out sooner but for his fear that if Joyce 'made a name someday' it would be remembered against him. His fears came true. When Joyce came to write *Ulysses,* he set the opening scenes in the tower, with 'stately, plump' Buck Mulligan carrying out his daily ablutions. Gogarty was the model for Buck Mulligan and he was not pleased with the honour Joyce paid him.

On one side of the tower is a rocky bathing place known as the **Forty Foot**, not for its depth but because the 40th Regiment of Foot of the British army was stationed here. It used to be the preserve of men only who delighted in 'skinny-dipping', but female liberation has come to the Forty Foot and now the swimmers – both male and female – are more modestly dressed. These toughened bathers brave the icy waters of the Irish Sea all year round.

Further south along the coast is **Dalkey,** once a medieval walled town and important trading post. The town has captured the imagination of several writers – Flann O'Brien (Brian Nolan), the brilliant satirical novelist, used it in *The Dalkey Archives,* while playwright Hugh Leonard set his play *Da* there. In recent years, Dalkey has become the Beverly Hills of Ireland with the beautiful houses tucked away behind high

Top, *Sandycove, with the Martello Tower which houses the James Joyce Museum, to the right of it is the white block of architect Michael Scott's house built in the 1930s.* Middle and bottom, *views along the coast of Sandycove and Killiney Bay.*

walls or chipped out of the Dalkey hillside and owned by musicians such as Bono from U2 and Chris de Burgh, writer Maeve Binchy, or film directors like Neil Jordan. But for all that the atmosphere of Dalkey has not changed. It is still a charming place to ramble or sit and watch for stars. Behind the village is Dalkey Hill, its disused quarry leaving a scarred cliff-face. A ridge leads from the quarry to a public park on **Killiney Hill** and offers breathtaking views of Dublin Bay and inland to the Wicklow mountains.

A short distance to the seaward side of Dalkey village is tiny **Coliemore Harbour**, packed with fishing boats, nets and tackle. Boats go from here to **Dalkey Island** a rocky, windswept island off **Sorrento Point**. Perched on one end of this little island is another **Martello Tower**, as well as a ruined early Christian church dedicated to **St Begnet**.

On the northernmost tip of Dublin Bay is **Howth Head** which comes to a point at the Baily lighthouse. Together with **Dalkey Island** on the southernmost tip, it curves round to form the sheltered harbour of Dublin Bay. Its height and commanding views across the bay and, on a clear day, across the Irish Sea to Wales, gave it military importance from the earliest times and wave after wave of invaders have left their mark here. According to legend a cairn on top of Howth Head marks the grave of an early Celtic chieftain. Centuries later Viking raiders must have realised how perfect a site this was as they nosed along the coast looking for somewhere to set up a trading post. They left evidence of their time here in the ruined **Howth Abbey** which Sigtrygg, the Norse king of Dublin, founded in 1042. Inside lies the tomb of Christian St Lawrence and his wife, ancestors of the Normans, the next wave of conquerors to come to Ireland. Hundreds of years later, the St Lawrence family still lives in **Howth Castle.**

On the northside of the head is **Howth Harbour**, once an important port but now overshadowed by the new marina and yachtclub beside it. Fishing boats still go out from the harbour, circling round **Ireland's Eye**, the tiny island almost in the mouth of the harbour, to reach the open sea. On the island is another **Martello Tower**, as well as the remains of the 6th century monastic settlement of **St Nessan**. But these days it is uninhabited except for the many birds who take sanctuary there.

Looking towards Dublin city from Howth, long stretches of sand and dunes catch the eye. These are the protected areas of **Dollymount Strand**, packed with Dubliners on warm summer days, and **Bull Island** – a sandy spit, topped by grassy dunes and joined by a wooden bridge to shore. In winter, the only visitors here are the thousands of birds who use this as a stop-off point.

Top and middle, a path winds around Howth Head giving views as far as Wales on a clear day, bottom, Howth Abbey founded by the Norse in 1042 with, in the distance, the harbour and Ireland's Eye, a bird sanctuary.

*L*einster is one of the four ancient provinces of Ireland encompassing the picturesque mountains of **Wicklow**, the slob-lands and sandy beaches of county **Wexford**, **Kilkenny** seat of the noble Butlers, and the rich grass-lands of **Kildare** and **Meath**, as well as the flatlands of **Louth**, **Offaly**, **Laois** and **Carlow**, and water-logged **Westmeath** and **Longford**.

WICKLOW

Wicklow is known for its stunning landscape – both tamed and wild. It covers part of the area once known as 'the Pale', a small shifting region which, from the 16th century onwards, was regarded as civilised and loyal to the British. The legacy of Anglo-Irish rule remains in the fine country houses and formal gardens of **Russborough** and **Powerscourt**. But these gracious estates are surrounded on all sides by a wilder Wicklow, one of rolling hills, high boglands, and deep glacial valleys that are home to dark lakes and spectacular waterfalls. In these distant valleys, such as **Glenmalure** and the **Glen of Imaal**, Irish rebels once took refuge, knowing that the Wicklow mountains would draw a curtain over their presence. And alongside them are glimpses of a much earlier Irish allegiance in the important monastic settlement at **Glendalough**.

Facing page, *the rush of the 122m high Powerscourt Waterfall is exhilarating. When King George IV visited Powerscourt House in 1821 the waterfall was dammed to provide an even more spectacular sight, and a viewing bridge erected. The king spent too long dining, however, and never made the journey to the falls – luckily for him, when the torrent of pent-up water was released it swept the bridge away. Powerscourt House was gutted in a fire in 1974, and it now contains a restaurant and shops. But its formal gardens are well worth visiting.*

This page, top, *Great Sugarloaf mountain in Wicklow rears its granite head over the surrounding countryside,* bottom, right, *the Wicklow mountains include miles of heather- and gorse-covered peat bog uplands, over 600m high.*

Glendalough

Glendalough or the 'Glen of the Two Lakes' is the site of a monastery founded by St Kevin during the 6th century. It was an important centre of learning and like other monasteries of its type would have been rich in treasures – gold chalices, finely worked shrine covers and illuminated manuscripts. Just how rich a site Glendalough was is clear from the number of raids made by Vikings in the 9th and 10th centuries and by the English in the 14th century. Despite this, however, the monastery continued in use to the 16th century.

Most of the early Christian buildings are clustered around the lower of the two lakes and include a 10th

Top, left, *aerial view of the 6th century monastic settlement at Glendalough with the 30m high round tower, also bottom, clearly visible.*

century **cathedral**, an 8th century **Celtic cross**, and **St Kevin's Church**, a tiny stone building with later additions such as the belfry. The 30m high **round tower** is characteristic of such sites. The doorway may have been set high in the tower so that the monks could withdraw with their treasures in times of attack.

The monastery lies at the mouth of a steep-sided glacial valley, containing two lakes, and scenery that is overwhelmingly beautiful. Paths lead around the **Upper Lake** through dense woods to the thundering waterfall. All around in the woods and cliffs of the Upper Lake are pilgrim shrines and even the ruins of St Kevin's original church, **Tempeall na Skellig**. But it is the atmosphere of peace at Glendalough – even at the height of summer – that most impresses one.

Top, right, paths lead around the Upper Lake through thick woods, steep mountain and waterfall. Bottom, the ruins of Tempeall na Skellig, St Kevin's original church.

Top, *Selskar Abbey destroyed by Oliver Cromwell,* middle and bottom, *Wexford is rumoured to have ninety-three pubs, some of them, like Macken's', double as funeral parlours.*

WEXFORD

Vikings founded the port of Wexford many centuries ago to the south of the River Slaney estuary. And the importance of the sea, both for trade and fishing, is clear from the way the town looks out to sea from behind its broad quays. Narrow winding streets and unexpected alleyways are remnants of the medieval town. Captured by the Normans in 1169, it had a spell as an English garrison town, but the tragedy of its history was the massacre of 1,500 of its townspeople by Oliver Cromwell at a spot known as the **Bull Ring**.
As a result of its troubled history Wexford and the surrounding county are dotted with tower houses, and crumbling castles and abbeys. **Duncannon Fort** was built in expectation of an attack by the Spanish Armada, the 15th century **Ballyhack Castle** guards Waterford estuary, and there are two 18th century Cistercian abbeys, **Dunbrody** and **Tintern**, which was established by a shipwrecked earl in gratitude for being washed ashore alive.
County Wexford has miles of sandy beaches at **Curracloe**, **Rosslare** and **Bannow**, while the mud flats to the north of the Slaney estuary provide winter shelter for thousands of the usual gulls and terns, but also pale-bellied Brent geese, whooper swans, and black-

tailed godwits. Endangered species such as Bewick's swans and Greenland white-fronted geese depend on Wexford's sloblands for their survival. Best bird-watching spots are **Carnsore Point**, the **Saltee Islands** or **Hook Head**.

Kilmore Quay

Many of Wexford's prettiest villages are scattered along its coast. **Kilmore Quay**, a picturesque fishing village, has a working harbour that is a tangle of masts and nets. It is part of the ancient barony of **Forth**, a remnant of Norman culture, where until early this century a dialect of medieval French called 'Yola' was still spoken.

Hook Head

Hook Head Peninsula juts south protecting the mouth of the River Barrow and the town of New Ross on its banks. Guiding sailors round this outcrop – which is rich ground for fossil-hunters – is the striped landmark of **Hook Head lighthouse,** the oldest lighthouse in Europe.

Top right, *Wexford Main Street,* middle, *Kilmore Quay harbour, a tangle of masts and fishing nets,* bottom, *Hook Head lighthouse, the oldest in Europe.*

THATCHED COTTAGES

From the 17th century onwards thatched cottages with their fresh whitewashed walls and tiny windows were a common sight in rural Ireland. Most have now been replaced by modern bungalows with tiled roofs, but some thatched cottages are still to be found in the southeast and west of the country. Each area has its own distinctive style – those in Donegal and the west coast where Atlantic gales sweep in have thatches secured with ropes and weights in a criss-cross pattern. The materials used differ too according to what is available locally – in the west and south heather might be used, while in coastal areas marram grass is more common. Those in Kilmore Quay use beautiful golden straw.

The style of thatched cottages varies from region to region, this page, those in Kilmore Quay in County Wexford use golden-coloured straw.

SOUTHEAST IRELAND

KILKENNY

The lush farmlands of **Kilkenny**, watered by the rivers Barrow and the Nore, drew settlers early in Irish history and the remains of their castles and abbeys are to be found everywhere. More recently a fresh wave of settlers – artists, craftspeople and writers have been drawn by its unspoiled landscape. Pretty villages, such as medieval walled **Thomastown** and **Graigue-managh** on the Barrow, dominated by **Duiske Abbey**, lie around every bend in the road.

The Castle

Kilkenny Castle stands on a hill overlooking the River Nore and the narrow streets of the ancient town of Kilkenny. Four medieval abbeys, and **St Canice's Cathedral** – with its original 6th century tower – cluster there as testament to the city's former importance. The Norman earl, Strongbow, left a fort on the site of the castle after he captured the town in 1169. The walled city and castle followed and the great Butler family, earls of Ormonde, held the castle and rich lands from 1391 until 1715, when their property was confiscated for rebelling against the English. Kilkenny's glory days were over but the castle stands as a memorial.

Top, right, *detail from stained glass window in the 13th century Black Abbey, just one of four abbeys in Kilkenny city,* bottom, *Kilkenny Castle, home to the Butlers, earls of Ormonde, was host to parliament from 1631.*

Jerpoint Abbey

A few miles out of Thomastown is the fine ruin of **Jerpoint Abbey**. Dating from 1158, it was founded by the King of Ossory, Donal Mac Giolla Phádraig, for the Benedictines. By 1180, Cistercian monks from a monastery in Baltinglass in County Wicklow had colonised it. After the Reformation the abbey's land was leased to the Earl of Ormonde. It conforms to the typical design for a Cistercian abbey – built around a quadrangle with arcaded walkways on three sides, and a church on the fourth side. In the 15th century parts of the abbey were rebuilt – and the fine sculptures of animals, plants and figures in the cloisters were added. On opposite sides of the same pillar are a bishop and an abbot, a knight bearing the arms of Earl of Ormonde and his wife, tentatively named as Sir Piers Butler and Margaret Fitzgerald.

Top, left, *the tower in the north corner of Jerpoint Abbey was probably added in the 15th century,* bottom, left and right, *fine carvings of saints, knights, animals and plants decorate the abbey cloisters.*

CARLOW

Southwest of Dublin, **Carlow** is Ireland's smallest inland county and largely given over to agriculture. But it also has a scattering of fine country houses such as **Dunleckney Manor** near **Bagnelstown**, **Castletown Castle** at **Clonegal**, and beautiful gardens, many of which are open to the public, such as **Altamont Gardens** near **Kilbridge** or **Lisnavagh Gardens** at **Rathvilly**.

Browne's Hill Dolmen

This enormous stone structure dates from 3300-2900BC, and its capstone – lying horizontally across the other stones – weighs approximately 101 tonnes and is 1.9m², making it the largest in Europe. No one has yet solved the mystery of how it was lifted into place. Typically, the capstone would be tilted upwards at the front, standing on two portal stones roughly the same size.

Portal dolmens like this as well as passage graves dating from the Neolithic period dot the Irish countryside. These dolmens were used as communal burial places and it has been suggested that they had a place in religious rites, perhaps even in human sacrifice.

Top, right and bottom, *Browne's Hill dolmen dates from 3300-2900BC and is the largest dolmen in Europe.*

KILDARE

County Kildare falls into the Pale, that area of land 'civilised' by English colonisation. And so it comes as no surprise to find grand country estates such as **Castletown House** here, but Kildare also has rich grasslands, boglands associated with mythic Ireland, and a scattering of beautiful early Christian crosses that are worth tracking down.

St Brigid's Cathedral

St Brigid is one of Ireland's most important saints, though she is probably an amalgam of a pre-Christian goddess and a later Christian Brigid. According to legend, Brigid was sold into slavery by her father, but returned to him as a servant when she was released. She then founded the first convent in Ireland. It became a centre of learning, producing illuminated manuscripts and precious books. **St Brigid's Cathedral** which dominates the town of Kildare is believed to have been built on the site of her 5th century monastery.

Parts of the building date from the 12th century, but it was heavily restored in the 15th and again in the 19th

Top, left and bottom, St Brigid's Cathedral, in the centre of Kildare, built on the site of the saint's 5th century monastery.

century. The 12th century **round tower**, with its ornate Romanesque doorway, is well worth climbing for its fine views.

Irish National Stud

Kildare is famous for its horses, bred and trained in the grasslands of the **Curragh**. Here too are the race course and many studs, including the **National Stud** set up by Colonel Hall Walker in 1900. An eccentric man, Hall Walker believed firmly in horoscopes and their influence on a horse's success. The stalls in the stable yards are built according to his astrological beliefs. Whether he was right or not, the National Stud has been remarkably successful and its horses can be seen at the race events that run from April to September.

Japanese Gardens

In the grounds of the National Stud, between 1906-1910 Colonel Hall Walker also laid out the **Japanese Gardens**, with the help of a Japanese gardener, Tasa Eida. The gardens symbolise 'the life of man' and you can literally walk the path of life from birth via marriage or bachelorhood and finally through the Gateway to Eternity.

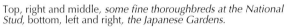

Top, right and middle, *some fine thoroughbreds at the National Stud,* bottom, left and right, *the Japanese Gardens.*

Top, *Castletown House, the central block and colonnades introduced the Palladian style to Ireland,* middle left, *the main staircase, unfinished for 40 years, stands in a separate chamber, decorated by the foremost craftsmen of the time,* right and bottom, *details from the Long Gallery, 24m long and decorated in the Pompeiian style.*

Castletown House

One of the most splendid houses in Ireland, **Castletown**, in the village of **Celbridge**, is credited with introducing the Palladian style to Irish architecture. Even at the time it was being built, Castletown was envisaged as a sort of national monument. Commissioned by William Conolly, Speaker of the Irish House of Commons, and, from 1716, Lord Justice, the house was an act of patriotism and political intent.

Conolly had made his money through buying and selling confiscated land after the Williamite wars. Fiercely proud of his Irishness – and now very wealthy – he was determined to foster Irish interests and national self-esteem. He employed the finest architect on the Continent, the Italian Alessandro Galilei who designed the Lateran Basilica in Rome. How much of the design is Galilei's, however, is uncertain. Certainly he designed the central block and it sparked a host of imitations. The pavilions and the interior are probably the work of Edward Lovett Pearce who took over the project in 1724.

After Conolly's death, his widow concentrated on a series of strange famine relief works in the demesne – **Conolly's Folly**, the **Wonderful Barn** and **Batty's Langley Lodge.** But much of the interior had to wait until 1758 and the arrival of Lady Louisa Lennox, the wife of Conolly's great nephew. She employed Simon Vierpyl, the stone mason, to install the great cantilevered **staircase**, the famous Italian stuccodores, the Francinis, to carry out the exquisite plasterwork in the **stair hall**. She was also responsible for the **print room**, the earliest example in existence. Lady Louisa lived long and loved Castletown. She died as she wished, seated in a tent on the front lawn so that her last sight was her home.

THE MIDLANDS

OFFALY

The **Grand Canal** runs through the flatlands of **County Offaly** on its way to the great River Shannon, south are the foothills of the **Slieve Bloom** mountains, while east and west is the bogland that provides the country with its primary source of fuel.

Clonmacnois Monastery

Clonmacnois sits at a bend of the River Shannon, and was founded by St Ciarán in 545 after he abandoned his cell on an island in Lough Ree. The monastery grew in size and reputation to become, for a time, the most important religious site in the country. Its graveyard supposedly holds the graves of seven kings of Tara, plus the last High King Rory O'Connor, and many of ancient Ireland's greatest heroes (many early Christian graveslabs still remain). It was also a centre of learning – the 12th century *Book of the Dun Cow*, now in the **Royal Irish Academy** in Dublin, came from its *scriptorium*. But the monastery's power and wealth drew unwelcome attention from Viking raiders – between 841 and 1204 it was burned twenty-six times. Finally, in 1552 the English garrison stationed in Athlone looted the monastery. Clonmacnois never recovered.

Just how powerful Clonmacnois once was is clear from what remains – two **round towers**, a Norman **castle** built to compensate an abbot for damage done to his property, three **high crosses**, **churches** and a **cathedral**.

Right, a round tower at Clonmacnois monastery, said to have been built in 964, and rebuilt after lightening struck in 1134.

Birr

Birr town is an elegant Georgian place with wide and gracious streets, built around **Birr Castle**, which was home to the Parsons family, who later became the earls of Rosse. The castle – still lived in by the family – was built in the early 17th century and sits above a waterfall that runs into one of two rivers on the estate. The gardens were laid out in the early 19th century and boast an artificial lake, formal gardens with hornbeam *allées,* the highest box hedges in the world and over a thousand varieties of tree and shrub. But most famous of all are the remains of a 16.5m-long telescope – the largest in the world at one time. Charles Parsons, third Earl of Rosse and a noted scientist, had it built in the grounds in 1845 and its 183cm diameter wide reflector, now in the Science Museum in London, aided his investigation of the spiral nebulae. The walls that supported the telescope still stand but the telescope itself has been dismantled.

MEATH

Up until the 16th century, **County Meath**, along with neighbouring **County Westmeath**, made up the fifth province of Ireland. Fed by the Boyne River, which led early settlers inland from the coast, Meath is rich and green countryside and consequently became the place from where the High King once ruled Ireland.

Trim Castle

In the centre of the fine medieval town of **Trim**, sits the ruins of a vast castle, abandoned in the 1650s. Boarded on three sides by walls up to 3.4m thick, and by the Boyne river on the fourth, it sits where an earlier motte with a wooden tower was erected, burnt, rebuilt and demolished, all before 1212.

Bective Abbey

Further north along the Boyne, a Cistercian abbey was founded in 1150 by the King of Meath. The abbot held a seat in Parliament and consequently **Bective Abbey** was a powerful one. The ruins date from the 12th century when the abbey was rebuilt – the **chapter house**, fragments of the domestic buildings and doorways of the **south wing**. In the 15th century, the buildings were fortified, the **cloister** rebuilt, the **tower** and **great hall** added. The abbey was suppressed in 1536.

Hill of Tara

Few places in Ireland are as central to Irish history and legend as the royal hill of **Tara**. Here, the High King held court and the rituals of kingship were enacted. And according to legend, it was on the nearby **Hill of Slane** in the 5th century that St Patrick chose to challenge the pagan might of Tara and its High King Laoghaire. The encounter was significant – Laoghaire submitted to St Patrick's god and Ireland's conversion to Christianity began in earnest.

But Tara's religious significance actually dates back earlier than that, to pre-history and the cult of the priest kings which grew into that of the high kings.

Excavations reveal that Tara holds many Iron Age burial sites, ring forts and earthworks. From ground level the hill is disappointing – little more than a grassy mound – but from the top it commands impressive views eastwards to the coast, north to the Mourne mountains and south to Wexford.

Top, left, the Lia Fáil, or Stone of Destiny, the inaugural stone, it was said to roar when a rightful king stood on it, bottom, the Hill of Tara, showing the ring fort known as 'Cormac's House'.

Newgrange

Newgrange is one of three prehistoric sites in the complex known as **Brú na Boinne**, in the bend of the Boyne beyond Slane, the others being **Dowth** and **Knowth**. All are passage graves – a large burial chamber beneath a raised mound – but Newgrange is acknowledged as the most important Stone Age site in Europe. A vast circular mound, roughly 9m high by 104m in diameter, its great stone slabs are decorated with intricate spirals, which may have some religious or astronomical meaning. Inside the mound a stone-lined tunnel leads to a chamber 6m high with a corbelled roof. On the morning of the winter solstice, a slit in one of the roofslabs channels the rising sun's rays along the tunnel and into the chamber, making it glow with light.

Not surprisingly, this ancient site appears in many Celtic legends.

The Stone Age tomb of Newgrange, top, right, *at dawn on the winter solstice, a slit above the entrance focuses the sun's rays along the inner tunnel to light up the main chamber,* bottom, *the mound stands 9m high.*

LOUTH

After many turns and bends the river Boyne finally reaches the sea at **Drogheda**, a Viking town which perches on the river banks. Long sandy beaches edge the coastline of this county, while in the north at **Carlingford**, just as the famous song says, the mountains of **Mourne** 'sweep down to the sea'.

Drogheda

The Vikings built a settlement on each bank of the Boyne and the bridge which joins the two gave the town its name, *Droichead Atha*, meaning 'Bridge of the Ford'. By the 14th century Drogheda had grown to rival Dublin, even hosting parliamentary sittings. Fragments of this medieval city survive. Oliver Cromwell passed through Drogheda in 1649, massacring 2,000 of the garrison, the survivors were sent into slavery in Barbados. But most of the town dates from the more peaceful days of the 18th and 19th century.

Mellifont Abbey

The first Cistercian abbey in Ireland, **Mellifont Abbey**, was founded in 1142 by St Malachy, the Archbishop

Top, left, Drogheda town on the banks of the Boyne river, bottom, remnants of the first Cistercian abbey in Ireland at Mellifont.

of Armagh. At the height of its reign, and as the Mother house of the Order, **Mellifont** ruled as many as thirty-eight other monasteries in Ireland. The monastery was disbanded under the dissolution of the abbeys by King Henry VIII in 1539. The ruins show the scale and grandeur of the original building.

Muiredach's Cross

Not far from Mellifont Abbey is **Monasterboice**, a much smaller monastery which is famous for its two **Celtic crosses** and **round tower**. **Muiredach's Cross** is the smaller and more perfect of the two. Both crosses are decorated with scenes from the Bible worked in relief on every side. Most have been identified – included are the Last Judgement, the Wise Men bearing gifts to the baby Jesus and the Crucifixion.

Founded in 521, Monasterboice was abandoned sometime after 1122. It contains the tallest round tower in Ireland, although this was burnt in 1097 and the manuscripts and treasures it contained lost in the fire.

Right, the east face of the 10th century High Cross known as Muiredach's Cross shows biblical scenes such as David killing the Lion and the Ascension, bottom, the interior of one of two churches at Monasterboice.

*T*he six counties that make up the Province of **Munster** are each wildly different in landscape, with lush **Tipperary**, picturesque **Waterford**, the prettiness of **Cork** and its bays, the beautiful lakes of **Kerry**, historic **Limerick** and the limestone flats of **Clare**.

TIPPERARY

Perhaps it is because of **Tipperary** that Ireland is famed for its greenness. The River Suir winds through the vast plain of the **Golden Vale** watering this rich green pasture for the dairy herds, while to the south the **Galtee** and the **Comeragh mountains** rise into view.

Rock of Cashel

Standing high above the surrounding plateau, the dramatic **Rock of Cashel** – all turrets and towers – is awe-inspiring. This cluster of medieval ecclesiastic buildings includes **Cormac's Chapel**, a **cathedral**, a **round tower**, a **tower house**, and the **Hall of the Vicars** with **St Patrick's High Cross** which, it is said, was the coronation stone for the Munster kings.
The rock was the site of a 4th century fortification for the Munster kings and, as late as the 10th century, Brian Boru, the Munster king who succeeded in uniting Ireland under his rule, was crowned here and called Cashel his capital. Cormac's Chapel dates from the early 12th century and both doorways, with their intricate carvings of animals and human heads, pillars and flutings, are superb examples of Romanesque stonework. Inside, a sarcophagus is believed to have been the tomb of Cormac, the king, bishop and scholar. The round tower could be as old as 10th century, while the cathedral, Gothic in design, dates from the 13th century.

Top, left, the spectacular Rock of Cashel with an early church, a vast cathedral, a round tower and a tower house and, middle, the 15th century Hall of the Vicars, bottom, intricate stone carvings of saints on an altar tomb in the cathedral.

Top, *Reginald's Tower in Waterford probably dates from the 12th century.*

WATERFORD

County Waterford is very picturesque, with craggy mountains to the north and a coastline of sandy bays and cliffs to the south. The River Suir continues south from Tipperary through Waterford county, tipping into the sea at the town of **Waterford**, an important port. The Vikings, Normans and Anglo-Irish have all left their mark on the countryside, scattering tower houses, castles and grand estates here and there. Waterford itself, like many other cities, owes its importance to the presence of a deep natural harbour at the mouth of a river that runs far inland to the rich southeast. The Vikings were the first to take advantage of these features when they established the town in 914. When Dermot MacMurrough, king of Leinster, invited the Anglo-Norman Earl of Pembroke to secure the strategically important town for him, it was as part of his tactics to become king of Ireland. However, the invitation had unforeseen consequences – leading eventually to the Anglo-Norman colonisation of Ireland. The medieval town flourished as a port and continued to do so up to the 19th century. The architecture of Waterford reflects its commercial past, there are areas of Georgian elegance, the long quays and narrow alleyways of Viking and medieval Waterford. The grimmier face of its commercial district, the quays, lined with cranes and cargo vessels, still bring relative prosperity to the area.

Reginald's Tower

The massive cylindrical structure of **Reginald's Tower** has had many incarnations. Supposedly established by Reginald the Dane in 1003, the present structure is more likely to date from the time of the Normans. It was here, according to legend, that the Earl of Pembroke, or Strongbow as he became known, claimed his reward for conquering Waterford for Dermot MacMurrough, King of Leinster. He was given Aoife, MacMurrough's daughter, in marriage, and so gained her inheritance and cemented a crucial alliance between Norman earl and Irish king – the first of its kind. In 1463, the town mint was housed here, while in the 19th century it became a prison. It is now the **City Museum.**

Waterford Crystal Factory

Waterford is known worldwide for its **Crystal**, beautifully crafted ornamental and functional pieces in handblown or cut glass. Established in 1783, the factory closed down in 1851. One hundred years later it re-opened and now visitors can watch as glassblowers produce these classic designs.

SOUTHWEST IRELAND

CORK

Cork is the largest county in Ireland. Along its indented coastline ports such as **Youghal**, **Kinsale**, **Crosshaven** and, of course, **Cork** city were once thriving trading spots. To the east the gentle countryside is good farming land, but to the west it grows wilder and its extravagant beauty – the mountain pass of **Gougane Barra**, the cliffs of **Mizen Head**, rocky peninsulas, sheltered sandy bays – have attracted artists and craftsworkers from across the world to settle here.

Cork City

Cork prides itself on being the second city of Ireland. The old city sits high up an estuary on a flat island surrounded by the **River Lee,** which has brought it so much wealth through trade. On the facing banks the evidence of a newer Cork sprawls.

Cork was first settled by St Finbarr who built an abbey and school in the 7th century where the **cathedral** now stands. Inevitably, as with most Irish cities, the Vikings followed in the 9th century and the Normans in the 12th century. Much of the city was destroyed in the Siege of Cork in 1690 by Williamite forces. But the centuries following were ones of expansion – trade brought great wealth and the city grew fast. Many of the fine 18th and 19th century houses were financed by this prosperity. More recently, the city suffered in the fight for independence and the Civil War.

Top right, *Cork City is a jumble of spires and towers,* bottom left, *the pretty Georgian church of St Anne's Shandon where visitors can climb the tower to ring the bells,* and right, *the River Lee cuts around the island of the city centre.*

Top left and right, *Cork City Gaol is now a museum with a comprehensive history of the Republican movement and cameos of life inside*, bottom left, *Pugin's cathedral in the picturesque port of Cobh.*

Cork City Gaol

Cork City Gaol is now a museum, recording the lives and beliefs of those who were once imprisoned there, many of them involved in the Republican movement in the early part of this century, as well as displaying archeological and geological finds. Cork played a large part in the Anglo-Irish and Civil wars – Michael Collins, Commander in Chief of the Irish government forces was a Corkman – and the city was sacked by the Black and Tans, an infamous regiment of the British army, causing over £2.5 million of damage. They murdered the mayor of Cork, Thomas MacCurtain, in March 1920, while his successor Mayor Terence MacSwiney, who was jailed as a Republican, died on hunger strike in Brixton Prison in London in October 1920.

Cobh Village

The pretty harbour town of **Cobh** is dominated by its cathedral, built by Pugin in the Gothic style. It was also the last port of call for many transatlantic liners – thousands of Irish emigrants embarked at Cobh, the ill-fated *Titanic* stopped here, as did the *Lusitania*, torpedoed off the Irish coast by a German submarine in 1915. Many of the victims are buried in the old church cemetery. But Cobh has happier associations too – as a Victorian health spa such as Bath or Brighton in England; and as a yachting centre the Cobh yacht club opened here in 1720.

Timoleague Abbey

Inland on a muddy estuary of the River Argideen sits the tiny village of **Timoleague**. It is dominated by the ruins of a **Franciscan Abbey**, founded in 1312 by Donal Glas MacCarthy, a member of the most powerful family in the area, whose burial place it is. After the dissolution of the monasteries by King Henry VIII in the 1600s, the friars returned in 1604 and carried out many repairs and alterations. However, when an English army burnt down the monastery and village of Timoleague in 1642, it was abandoned. Remaining are a church, claustral buildings, a graveyard, high crosses, crooked tombstones and splendid views.

Top, right, *Timoleague Abbey, founded in 1312 and eventually abandoned in the 17th century,* bottom, *splendid views south from Healy Pass.*

Kinsale

The bay of **Kinsale** is well-protected by a spit of land that curves in from the west into the harbour. Behind this finger of land Kinsale town climbs upwards through the narrow streets that overlook the busy port. Such a natural harbour and southerly port had huge strategic importance during Ireland's troubled past. It was the site of the disastrous Battle of Kinsale in 1601 which ended the power of the Gaelic lords and resulted in the 'Flight of the Earls' when they fled to Europe, leaving their lands to the English. But these days, Kinsale is better known for its beautiful tile-fronted houses, its gourmet restaurants and its pretty marina.

St Multose Church

Built on the site of a monastery founded by St Multose who is believed to be commemorated in a statue over the west door of the church. The present church dates back to the 12th century – the unusual tower and its Romanesque door still survive. The **chancel** was added in 1560, with other additions dating back to the 19th century – including the **stocks** in the porch.

The Old Courthouse

When the liner *The Lusitania* was torpedoed by a German submarine off Kinsale in 1915, 1,198 people died. Whether the liner was carrying gunpowder as the Germans claimed or just its unfortunate passengers as the Americans claimed, the event is credited with precipitating the United States into the First World War. The inquest was held in the **Old Courthouse** and it stands now as a memorial to the event.

Top left to right, the 12th century St Multose Church with its unusual tower, and the Old Courthouse which commemorates the lives lost aboard the Lusitania. Middle and bottom, Kinsale's narrow cobbled streets, excellent restaurants and pubs attract Irish and foreign food-lovers, especially during its Gourmet Festival in early October.

Top, *Drombeg stone circle is one of the best preserved sites of its kind,* bottom, right, *nearby is a hunting stop, with the remains of a hut and cooking place.*

Drombeg Stone Circle

When **Drombeg** stone circle was excavated a cremated body was found in an urn in the centre of the seventeen standing stones, indicating that the circle may have had some ritual function. The westernmost stone lies flat with what looks like a human foot or a cup carved on it. The circle is believed to date from the 2nd century and is just one of many that are scattered across Ireland, relics of Neolithic man. There are many theories as to the function of these stone circles – they may have been prehistoric 'observatories' used to study the movement of the skies, or the site for religious rites. Nearby the remains of an old hunting stop remain – there is a hut and a cooking place.

Top, *a suspension bridge links the lighthouse off Mizen Head with the mainland,* middle, left, *the peninsula juts far out into the Atlantic Ocean,* and bottom, *the wide sweep of Barleycove Bay.*

Mizen Head

The long southerly peninsula jutting out into the Atlantic Ocean above **Roaring Water Bay** in County Cork is **Mizen Head**. The cliffs rising steeply out of the water make this dangerous water for boats, and many have been shipwrecked in **Dunlough Bay** to the north. A lighthouse beams out its warning to sea traffic from an island linked to Mizen Head by a suspension bridge. All around is wild and desolate scenery, rich with prehistoric burial sites, ring forts and medieval castles. On Mizen Head itself are the remains of **Three Heads Castle**, one of twelve castles built along this peninsula in the 15th century by the O'Mahoney clan. Along its southern side, the cheerful villages of **Schull** and **Ballydehob** teem with visiting artists, jewellery makers, weavers and writers who have fallen in love with the beautiful views and its residents' relaxed outlook and stayed on.

Barleycove Beach

This wonderful stretch of sandy beach tucked in behind **Mizen Head** is washed by the Gulf Stream and so can boast some of the warmest waters in Ireland, that and its long Atlantic rollers make it popular with surfers.

Top, *Bantry House, built in 1720 and added to over the centuries,* middle, right, *the royal blue dining room, with portraits by Allan Ramsey,* and bottom, *the Gobelin room is reputed to contain a panel that belonged to Louis Philippe, the Duc d'Orleans.*

Bantry House

No other country house in Ireland commands quite such spectacular views as **Bantry House**. Sitting at the head of a narrow inlet overlooking the waters of Bantry Bay, it gazes out at **Whiddy Island** and the majestic **Caha Mountains**. The original three-storey house was built in 1720, but was bought in 1746 by Richard White – a Whiddy Island farmer who had amassed a fortune, possibly through smuggling. He also acquired much of the land on Beare peninsula. His grandson, also Richard White, was knighted for remaining loyal to the British when a French fleet arrived at Bantry Bay in 1796 to join the United Irishmen's uprising. During his lifetime he added a two-storey extension on to the house with bowed ends and a six bay front looking on to the sea. But it was another earl, a traveller and art connoisseur, who collected the extraordinary treasures the house now contains, priceless tapestries – Gobelins and Aubussons – paintings and furniture. He had to extend the house considerably to accommodate his collection. The splendid terraced gardens rising uphill behind the house have recently been restored.

Top left and right, *the exotic gardens of Garnish Island where the sub-tropical growth is due to the Gulf Stream,* bottom, left, *one of the many seals to be found sunbathing on the rocks in Bantry Bay.*

Garnish Island

Just opposite **Glengariff** in **Bantry Bay** is a tiny island called **Garnish**. Up until 1910 this was a rocky outcrop like the mountains looking down on it from the mainland. John Allan Bryce, its owner, imported the topsoil and developed these stunning gardens, a miracle of lushness in a bare rocky area. There is an **Italian garden** designed by Harold Peto, a **Grecian temple** looking out to sea, a **Martello Tower** and a **Clock Tower**. It was here that the playwright and Nobel Prizewinner George Bernard Shaw wrote *St Joan*. The island was donated to the nation by Byrce's son.

Seal Island

The boatmen who take visitors to **Garnish Island** rarely forget to pay a visit to the rocky islands where seals like to lie and soak up the weather. Perhaps it is the warmer water that the Gulf Stream sweeps into Bantry Bay that pleases these animals so much.

KERRY

Nowhere in **Kerry** is far from water, either that of the Atlantic Ocean that rolls in around Kerry's many mountainous peninsulas or that of the many lakes around **Killarney**. It is spectacular scenery with Ireland's highest mountain, **Carrauntoohil**, jutting up out of the **MacGillycuddy Reeks** and contrasting with the gentler lands of the lakes and their islands. Perhaps it is the remoteness of Kerry that has kept the Irish culture so alive in this area – here, you will hear traditional music played in the pubs, get a chance to dance Irish style, hear Irish spoken in one of the *Gaeltacht* areas along the **Dingle** peninsula, and watch lace-makers at their craft.

Top and middle, right, *nuns in a convent in Kenmore village perfected a unique style of lace-making. Now it is to be found in the many craftshops, in the area,* bottom.

Kenmare

The tiny fishing town of **Kenmare** is surprisingly cosmopolitan with many tourists and foreign residents, but in the middle of the health food and tourist shops, the delicatessens and expensive restaurants, its own culture continues regardless. Traditional crafts such as lace-making, invented by the nuns at the local convent and so technically perfect it commanded huge prices, fill the tourist outlets and market day is still the most important day of the month. Local farmers drive their livestock to market, haggle long and loud and seal a deal by spitting into the palm of their right hand and shaking on it.

Sir William Petty, Oliver Cromwell's surveyor general, established the town in the 1640s to serve his iron smelting plant near the River Finnihy. The iron was smelted with charcoal and consequently, the woods in this area were devastated. But it was the first Marquis of Lansdowne, the local landowner, who decided on the layout of the town in 1775 – it is designed in an X plan.

On market day the local farmers gather to exchange gossip and strike bargains.

Top, *the wonderful lakes of Killarney drew tourists as far back as 1756, when Lord Kenmare funded four major roads to encourage more visitors,* bottom, right, *Moll's Gap where centuries of glacial erosion has smoothed out great boulders.*

Lakes of Killarney

All the landscape in this part of Ireland owes its beauty to the glaciers of the last Ice Age over a million years ago. One sheet of ice drove south from the midlands, another went north from **Bantry**, yet another passed north through the **MacGillycuddy Reeks** and the mountains around **Killarney**. Twenty thousand years ago as the ice shrank back, it scooped out the three deep and spectacular lakes of Killarney. The **Upper Lake** was literally gouged out, while the **Middle** and **Lower** lakes were formed by the layers of limestone that had lain beneath the ice dissolving in the thaw. Elsewhere, the glaciers left debris in their wake at the **Gap of Dunloe** and east of **Lough Currane**, and wore away gigantic boulders and rocks at **Moll's Gap.** Today the mountains are covered in purple heathers and a quarter of all the rare Irish plants are to be found here. From May to July the hillsides and damper areas yield many Mediterranean-Lusitanian plants such as Butterworths and Saxifrages, while in July and August American oddities such as blue-eyed grasses and unusual rushes appear.

Top, left, *fishing trawlers in Dingle harbour are as likely to be taking tourists to view the sights as fishing*, top, right, *the village of Dingle is packed with colour-washed houses, lively pubs and good restaurants*, bottom, left, *Slea Head at the tip of the Dingle peninsula points out to the Blasket Islands, uninhabited since 1953.*

Dingle Village

Dingle was once Kerry's main port and working fishing boats still crowd the little harbour. Some take visitors to see Dingle's latest attraction, a friendly dolphin named *Fungi*, who likes to swim out to meet his visitors. All around this peninsula are ancient sites, monasteries, Celtic crosses and ruins, while the poverty and hardships of the locals and the islanders from the **Blasket Islands** just off **Slea Head** in the early part of this century are well-documented in Thomas O'Crohan's compelling book *The Islandman* and in the grim memoirs of islandwoman Peig Sayers. The islands were evacuated in 1953.

Dingle is for the most part a *Gaeltacht* or Irish-speaking area, one of the few rural places in Ireland where this ancient language has not died out. Alongside the language, Irish music and dance also flourish here and can usually be found in any pub on any night of the week.

Top, *Inch beach, a five kilometre-long sandy spit, backed by dunes,* bottom, right, *the Conor Pass winds 305m up from Dingle town to the northern side of the peninsula.*

Inch

At **Inch** a five kilometre sandy bar, backed by sandy dunes, stretches out almost halfway into the upper part of **Dingle Bay**. Exposed and constantly shifting with the shifts in winds, the dunes provide a habitat for rare and specialised communities of plants which have had to adapt to their conditions in order to survive. Some unfurl their leaves only when it rains, others take up to thirteen years to flower and reseed.

Marram grass holds the dunes together with its deep roots, while sea holly, with its thick spiky leaves and blue tinged flowers attracts butterflies. Bird's foot trefoil, clover, yellow seaside pansies and kidney vetch and even the rare and endangered orchid, lady's tresses, can be found in this area. It is also rich in birdlife with ringed plovers, who come to eat the sand hoppers, diving gannets, gulls and shags filling the shoreline.

Conor Pass

The **Conor Pass** winds round from **Dingle** town to the northern side of the peninsula along a 305m high cliffside road that runs between Brandon Mountain and Stradbally Mountain, giving unmissable views over the area.

Kilmakedar Church

A fine Romanesque church built on the site of the earlier church of St Mael Cathair. A grandson of the king of Ulster, Mael Cathair was probably a missionary to Kerry, and he died here in 636. The **church** had a corbelled roof, influenced perhaps by **Cormac's Chapel** on the **Rock of Cashel**, and consists of a **nave** and **chancel**. Inside a **stone** is inscribed with the Latin alphabet – a reminder of the early Christian settlements which had schools where children were taught to read and write. **The east window** is known as *'cró na snáthaide'* or 'eye of the needle' and pilgrims were supposed to squeeze through it to be saved. This stone was known for its healing properties, and was still used as recently as 1970. In the graveyard stands a carved early **sundial**, while nearby is **St Brendan's House**, probably a priest's residence.

Dunbeg Fort

Most of this 8th or 9th century promontory **fort** has fallen into the sea, but what remains is impressive. Four defensive banks surround a stone wall and the entrance passage through it has a 'dog hole' at ground level. Inside are the remains of a **house** and a **beehive hut**, and a **souterrain** leads from here to the outer defenses.

The Gallarus Oratory

The most perfect example of about twenty such oratories in Ireland, **Gallarus Oratory** is thought to have been built in the 9th or 10th century. It shows the transition from round beehive huts, such as at **Dunbeg**, to the rectangular churches found later.

LIMERICK

The city of Limerick guards the head of the Shannon estuary with the fine 13th century **King John's Castle**. Established by the Vikings, Limerick fell into the hands of the Irish led by the High King Brian Boru in the 10th century, and became the headquarters of the O'Brien clan. The Normans came next, fortifying the town and a relative peace reigned until Oliver Cromwell's forces captured the castle in 1651. Forty years later, when the Catholic King James II lost the crucial Battle of the Boyne in 1690 most of his supporters surrendered. But Limerick continued to fight under the Irish hero Patrick Sarsfield. A year later the city could hold out no longer and the infamous Treaty of Limerick was signed, allowing Catholics only minimal rights. According to legends, 'before the ink was dry' the English broke the agreement and introduced extreme anti-Catholic laws. Ever since Limerick has had the reputation of being a strongly nationalist town.

King John's Castle

Completed in 1202, it is a five-sided castle reinforced with four sturdy towers, one of which was replaced by a bastion in 1611. It now contains an **interpretative centre** of the history of Limerick.

Lough Gur

Around the shores of the horseshoe-shaped **Lough Gur** many Stone Age remains have been found including ring forts and huts, a finely crafted bronze shield from 700BC and a gallery grave. But most spectacular is the huge **standing stones** ringed in an almost perfect circle. Little is known of exactly how it would have been used but its purpose was undoubtedly ritual.

Adare

Until the early 19th century **Adare** village was a near slum. Then the third Earl of Dunraven who was landlord of Adare Manor, now a hotel, initiated all sorts of rural improvements including the tidy streets of quaint thatched cottages which still stand today.

Facing page, top left, *views from Slea Head to the Great Blasket Island,* top right, *Kilmakedar Church which contains fine stone carvings and once had a corbelled roof,* middle, *the promontory fort of Dunbeg with four defensive banks surrounding its stone wall,* bottom, *Gallarus's Oratory, the most perfectly preserved example of these stonebuilt buildings.*

This page, top right, *King John's Castle, built by the Normans in 1202, guards the entrance to the Shannon river,* middle, *the great stone circle in the Stone Age settlement at Lough Gur,* bottom, *rows of pretty thatched cottages in Adare village.*

MIDWEST IRELAND

CLARE

The barren limestone pavements of the **Burren** in the north of **Clare** draw many botanists to this county, but there is much more to wonder at – the spectacular **Cliffs of Moher**, the beautiful golden beaches of **Fanore, Ballyvaughan** and **Lahinch**, and above all, the best traditional music and singing in the country in villages such as **Doolin** and **Milltown Malbay**.

Bunratty Castle

Built in 1460 by the MacNamara clan, **Bunratty Castle** stands on what was once an island on the north bank of the Shannon. As with many fortified buildings in Ireland, the Vikings and Normans had previously built defensive structures on the site – the Viking's moat is still visible, while the Normans built the first castle on the island. Recently restored, the sturdy rectangular keep houses a collection of furniture, tapestries and paintings dating from the 14th to the 17th century. The castle is now used for medieval style banquets and is surrounded by the **Bunratty Folk Park**, a reconstruction of a 19th century village.

Cliffs of Moher

These spectacular sandstone and shale cliffs run for eight kilometres, and rear up to 200m out of the sea. Constant lashing by the stormy Atlantic has eroded the soft rock and here and there stacks of harder rock stand alone offshore.

This page, top left, *Bunratty Castle on the Shannon river,* bottom, left, *the Great Hall,* bottom, right, *the private chapel.*

Facing page, *the ravaged Cliffs of Moher in north Clare.*

This page, top, *Poulnabrone Dolmen stands in the centre of the limestone region, the Burren.*

Facing page, top, *northwest Clare has stunning beaches and visitors can rent traditional cottages at the seaside village of Ballyvaughan,* middle, *Lisdoonvarna is full of pubs like the Matchmaker Bar where each September bachelors and spinsters take part in the matchmakers festival, while throughout the area pubs such as O'Connor's in Doolin,* bottom, *guarantee traditional music every night of the week.*

The Burren

The Burren is a 260 square kilometre table of porous limestone, formed beneath the sea, brought to the surface by earth shifts and cracked open by glaciers. It is an extraordinary landscape, bleak and barren in winter months, but blindingly bright under summer sunshine and yielding on close examination a wealth of plant and animal life.

Rainwater seeps through the porous rock to hollow out underground caves and tunnels, while temporary lakes, known as *turloughs*, appear after heavy rain, disappearing once the underground water system has absorbed them.

The surface of the limestone pavement has been eroded into grooves and pockets known as *clints* (a type of rock outcropping) and *grykes* (cracks in clints). Out of these slits of shelter, fed by under-ground waterways, spring an abundance of rare flow-ers – among them spring gentians and orchids – more usually found in the Mediterranean, Alpine and Arc-tic regions, and especially impressive in April and May, as well as some species of snails, orchids and ferns only found here. It is a botanist's heaven. How the Mediterranean varieties survive here is a mystery, but it may be that the limestone soaks up heat during summer, storing it so the area has a milder climate during winter, or it may be the effect of the Gulf Stream blowing in a mild, moist wind from the sea.

Poulnabrone Dolmen

Poised over the strange landscape of the **Burren** in northwest Clare, this unusually graceful portal dol-men is believed to date from 2500BC. Excavations in

1986 uncovered the bones of fourteen adults and six pieces, shards of pottery and stone artifacts.

Ballyvaughan

On the northern shore of the **Burren** and facing onto **Galway Bay** is the seaside village of **Ballyvaughan**, popular with tourists and those exploring the limestone features of the area. Hereabouts are examples of traditional Irish cottages, one-storey whitewashed buildings with tiny windows to protect the inhabitants from the Atlantic winds.

Lisdoonvarna

Every September **Lisdoonvarna** becomes the venue for a month-long festival of matchmaking. As recently as the 1950s farmers would come to town after harvest-time to look for rest and diversion and as often as not a wife. Arranged marriages were common in rural areas until quite recently with the matchmaker introducing the couple and negotiating agreement on the dowry. The tradition has changed somewhat but Lisdoonvarna in September is still busy with nervous farmers and shy women hoping to make a match. The festival grew out of the town's popularity as a spa resort, its waters are loaded with minerals and you can still take sulphur baths, drink at a pump-house, or have a sauna and massage.

Doolin

Doolin's claim to fame is that it is the heartland of music in Ireland. In summertime its pubs are thronged with musicians and singers, playing together informally in what are called 'sessions'. Who turns up to play and what they play or sing will depend on the night, the mood and the crowd.
To the outsider the session looks chaotic, but in fact there are rules and courtesies involved and visiting musicians must wait to be invited before they can sit in. Most instrumental music is dance music and at a good session it can be impossible to sit still.

Doolin Pier

The coastline at **Doolin** is bare and windswept with the limestone slabs of the Burren running down into the sea. From its pier, boats go out to the three **Aran Islands** where Irish is still spoken.

Aillwee Caves

The stalagmites and stalactites of the **Aillwee Caves** in the **Burren** throw awesome shadows in the underground lights. These and the amazing rock formations in the series of caverns are caused by the endless seepage of water draining through the porous limestone pavements of the Burren.

Facing page, *the spectacular caverns of stalagmites and stalactites at the Aillwee Caves.*

This page, *at Doolin on the northwest coast of Clare, the Atlantic waves hurl themselves at the inhospitable shore,* top, *while the limestone pavement of the Burren,* bottom, left, *comes to an abrupt end at the sea's edge.*

*The western province of **Connaught** is made up of the lively city of **Galway**, with a hinterland of bog that extends into **Mayo**. There's the lowlands of **Roscommon** and the rugged beauty of **Sligo** – known as Yeats's country – alongside the lakelands of **Leitrim**.*

GALWAY

Galway city is full of charm. It is the capital of the *Gaeltacht* or Irish-speaking region, but it is also a thriving industrial centre, a market centre and a crucial focus for the arts – theatre and film are strong, and many artists are drawn to the area. In recent years it has experienced a boom and its population, drawn by improved job prospects, has increased dramatically making Galway the fastest growing city in Europe. It also has a reputation as Ireland's alternative city, as a result the streets are full of buskers, fire-throwers, jewellery sellers and craftsworkers who set up stalls and sell their goods. But most of all the city is full of young people who study at the city's university, and in summertime in particular with the Galway Arts Festival and the Races, the place buzzes with life. Galway's position at the mouth of the Galway River and as a crossing point on the River Corrib, made it an important trading centre from early days. In the 13th century the Anglo-Norman de Burgo family seized the town and it became a powerful Norman colony ruled by fourteen families, which led to it being called the 'City of Tribes'. While much of Ireland was in a state of rebellion against the English crown in the 15th to 17th centuries, Galway remained loyal. The city grew rich and had strong trade links with France, Spain and Portugal. However, its loyalty to the crown was its downfall when Cromwell came to power and his forces besieged the town in 1652 for ninety days. The famine in the 1840, also struck the west of Ireland especially hard and the city of Galway only began to recover from economic depression and population decline in this century.

Facing page, top, *Lynch's Castle belonged to one of the fourteen tribes which ruled the city for many centuries,* bottom, left and right, *details of coats of arms carved in stone on the Castle's exterior walls.*

This page, top, left, *the Browne doorway in Eyre Square, a fragment remaining from the house of a rich Galway merchant,* right, top, *Spanish Arch down by the harbour,* right, bottom, *the row of terraced houses overlooking the harbour wall faces the ancient Claddagh district across the river.*

Lynch's Castle

The early 16th century tower house on the corner of busy **Shop Street**, now a bank, belonged to the most powerful family in the district, the Lynchs. It features Irish gargoyles and the arms of Henry VII and the Fitzgeralds of Kildare on the exterior.

Browne Doorway

Trade with the Continent once made Galway the wealthiest city in Ireland and vestiges of those days remain in the fine townhouses and castles that survive.
The **Browne Doorway** on the north of **Eyre Square** is one such lonely fragment – dated 1627, it features the arms of two powerful Galway families, the Lynchs and the Brownes.

Spanish Arch

Down near the harbour, the 16th century **Spanish Arch** has been given many fanciful histories, but it was most likely that it was designed to protect galleons unloading their expensive cargos of rum and wine. Attached to the Arch is some of the original medieval wall of the city.

The Long Walk

Through Spanish Arch a road runs along the mouth of the river as it feeds into the sea. Here, swans like to feed, and Galway Hookers, the traditional working boats of the region, with their distinctive rust red sails, are often to be found. On the far side of the river, the Claddagh, once the fishermen's quarter of the city has largely disappeared under modern apartments and 1930s housing, which replaced the thatched cottages. Once this area had its own king, a distinctive way of dress and spoke Irish. All that remains is the name, and the famous Claddagh ring, the wedding ring used by people of the area which has been dated back to as long ago as 1784.

Galway International Oyster Festival

For most of September, Galway devotes itself to that king of shellfish, the Galway Bay oyster. The city is packed with bands, Irish dancers, oyster sellers, and oyster eaters who take it Irish style – accompanied by pints of creamy Guinness. But most of all there is *craic* – the Irish for a brilliant time.

Ballinasloe October Fair

Horses are the business at this ancient fair in the first week of October. Dealers come from all over Ireland and England to buy and sell, and bartering is a serious game that must be given time – and preferably performed in front of an audience who can appreciate the quality of the participants' skill.

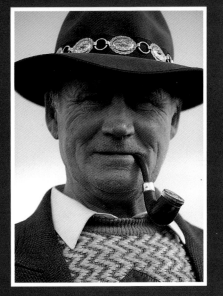

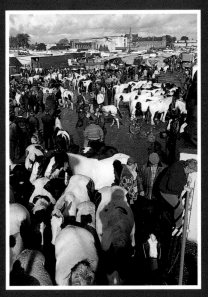

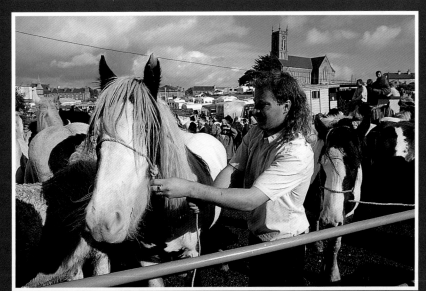

Top, *the neo-Gothic outline of Kylemore Abbey and, bottom, left, a short walk through the wooded grounds leads to the convent church.*

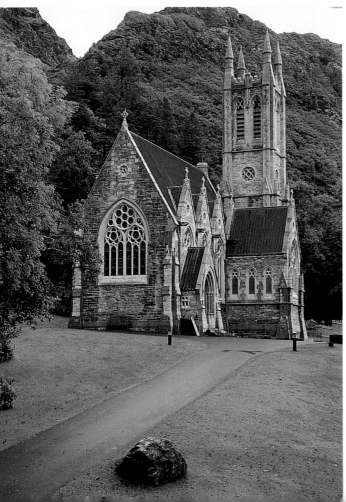

Clifden

It comes as a surprise that the tiny village of **Clifden** should be the capital of **Connemara**, that vaguely defined but beautiful area west and north of Galway. Behind **Clifden** the **Twelve Bens** mountains rise, while in front of it the **Owenglin River** joins the sea in a wide estuary. Most of Connemara is preserved in a national park, and the miles of empty bogland in soft browns, broken by small lakes, or pierced by the **Maam Turk** mountains and the Twelve Bens are virtually unspoilt.

Kylemore Abbey

Just east of Letterfrack in Connemara is **Kylemore Abbey**, a 19th century 'castle', built by a Liverpool merchant, whose Gothic style turrets and castellations throw fantastic shadows on Pollacappul Lough. A convent of Benedictine nuns settled there after the First World War, and set up a school. Its an unexpectedly green spot, a lush valley and rhododendron-covered slopes and a thick forest leading down to the Abbey's church, a mini copy of Norwich Cathedral.

Lough Corrib

This large island-studded lake divides County Galway in two, north to south. Inland lies fertile, well-farmed land, while to the west on the coast is wild Connemara country, fiercely beautiful and composed, it seems of nothing but rock and water. There are 365 islands on **Lough Corrib**, one island, known as **Inchagoill**, contains the oldest Christian monument – apart that is from the Roman catacombs**.**

Dunguaire Castle

Standing on a narrow finger of land jutting into **Kinvarra Bay**, **Dun Guaire Castle** is actually a fortified tower house – common in this area – dating from the 16th century. The castle is named after Guaire Aidhneach, King of Connaught in the 7th century, who had his royal seat here. Guaire's hospitality was staggering – one bard describes how 350 guests with 350 servants and their dogs were lavishly entertained for sixteen months. Today, the tradition continues with the Shannon Development Company staging medieval banquets in the restored tower.

Ross Errilly Abbey

Ross Errilly Abbey on the shores of **Lough Corrib** is one of the best-preserved and most accomplished of the Franciscan monasteries. Founded in 1351, most of the building dates from the 15th century and it is easy to imagine how this building must have looked. The **church** with its castellated **tower** has well-preserved windows, showing a cross-section of the styles in use in the 15th century. There are two sets of **cloisters**, one arcaded, with the **bakeroom** beyond, while the **kitchen** in the northwest corner of the buildings has a water-tank for fish, and an oven which protrudes into the **mill room** behind.

Top, right, *the vast stretch of Lough Corrib is populated with many islands,* middle, *Dunguaire Castle, a fine example of the fortified tower house,* bottom, *Ross Errilly Abbey, the largest of the Franciscan abbeys in Ireland.*

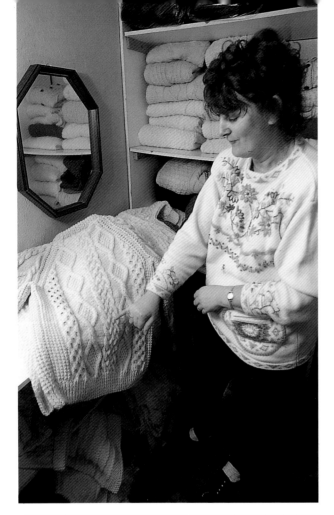

ARAN ISLANDS

At the mouth of **Galway Bay**, a few miles from **Doolin** or **Carraroe** by boat are three outcrops of rock, **Inishmore**, the largest and most visited island, unspoilt **Inishmaan**, and the smallest of the three, **Inisheer**.

Inishmore

All the Aran Islands are Irish-speaking, and many Irish children spend their summer holidays here to improve their accents as well as experience life in a *Gaeltacht* community. **Inishmore** is the largest of the islands and in summer is jammed with visitors, but it is still easy to slip away and explore on foot or by bicycle its seven ancient **churches** – for Inishmore is the site of the first and most important **monastery** in Ireland.

The island is a long slab of limestone, similar to the formation of the Burren in Clare, it slopes upwards on the southwest side to a height of 90 metres. However, most of the villages are grouped along the gentler northeast side of the island.

Dun Aenghus

This massive **ring fort** dates from sometime between 700BC and 100AD. Perched on the edge of a 60m drop to the sea, it seems as if some of **Dun Aenghus** has already taken the leap. Three rows of semicircular defenses make up the fort, the innermost with wall-walks and wall chambers, with a flat-headed entrance way. In the area leading up to the fort are thousands of stone stakes or *chevaux-de-frise*, a deterrent to anyone trying to storm the walls.

Top, left, *the Aran jumper, each family wears a different pattern,* bottom, left, *Dun Aenghus perches 60m above the sea,* bottom, right, *the peaceful harbour of Kilronan on the northerly side of the island.*

NORTHWEST IRELAND

MAYO

Mayo stretches from the island-sprinkled lakes of **Lough Mask** and **Lough Corrib** in the south to the northwest tip of **Belmullet**, and from **Achill Island** in the west to the **Ox Mountains** of **Sligo** and **Roscommon** in the east. Near **Westport**, an elegant Georgian town, **Croagh Patrick,** the pilgrimage mountain named for St Patrick, juts into the sky. Every year thousands of pilgrims climb to the chapel at the top in their bare feet.

In 1798, the French General Humbert and a thousand soldiers landed at **Kilcummin Strand** in North Mayo, taking **Killala** and **Ballina** and marching victorious to capture **Castlebar**. They were eventually defeated in County Longford and all those suspected of helping them were executed. Mayo was badly hit by the Great Famine of 1845-49, and thousands died or emigrated on the 'coffin ships' to America, leaving the land underpopulated and abandoning the homesteads which now stand in ruins.

Top, right, *a fine townhouse in Cong town,* bottom, *the ruins of Cong Abbey.*

Cong Abbey

The town of **Cong** sits on a narrow isthmus separating **Lough Mask** from **Lough Corrib**. Established as a monastery by St Feichin in the 7th century, Cong became the seat of the Kings of Connaught. In 1128 Turlough Mór O'Connor, King of Connaught, rebuilt Cong as an abbey for the Augustinians, and his son Ruaidhrí O'Connor, the last High King of Ireland, spent his final years here.

Only the **chancel** of the church survives, with some of the east side and a section of the **cloisters**, but these sections contain exquisite doors and window detailing in stone.

Facing page, top, the River Boyle runs smoothly through the town, middle and bottom, *views of the Cistercian monastery of Boyle.*

This page, left, window detailing in ancient Cong Abbey, bottom, left, a remnant from the 12th century, Romanesque door and cloister, bottom, right, now in ruins, the abbey was built for the Augustinian Order by Turlough Mór O'Connor, High King of Ireland in the 12th century.

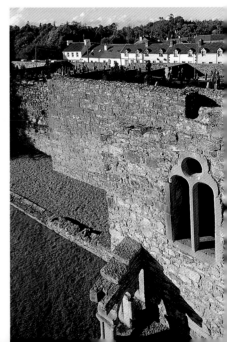

ROSCOMMON

This long strip of land, bound by the Shannon river down its east side, is the only inland county in Connaught. In the centre is **Roscommon** town with fine remains of the Anglo-Norman **Roscommon Castle**, to the east is the Georgian planned town of **Strokestown**, with at the end of its broad main avenue, **Strokestown House** and the **Famine Museum**.

Boyle

This pleasant town in northern Roscommon sits along the **Boyle River**. In the town centre stands the recently restored **King House**, a fine mansion built in the 1730s for the King family who later moved to the very grand **Rockingham** estate just outside Boyle. Rockingham was destroyed by fire in the 1950s and its lands now form part of the **Lough Key Forest Park**. Boyle also contains the remains of an early Cistercian abbey, founded by monks from Mellifont Abbey in 1161. The ruins of the nave show clearly two different styles of architecture – down one side are rounded Romanesque window arches, on the other those of the later Gothic period. Some of the windows also have elaborate leafed and figured capitals. The square **tower** dates from the 12th century as do two blocked up doorways on the east side. The other buildings date from the 16th and 17th century, though when Cromwell's forces occupied the monastery in 1659 they damaged it badly.

95

Left, top, *Benbulben mountain plays a part in Irish legend and the poetry of W B Yeats*, left, bottom, *Carrowmore stone circle with Knocknarea, the burial place of Queen Maeve, in the background,* right, *the high cross at Drumcliff where the poet W B Yeats's is buried.*

SLIGO

Few places in Ireland can count as many megalithic sites per square kilometre as **Sligo**, and these ancient monuments such as **Carrowkeel**, **Knocknarea** and **Carrowmore** have gathered many myths around themselves. The poet William Butler Yeats drew inspiration from the strangeness of this uninhabited landscape as did his brother the painter Jack Yeats.

Benbulben

This oddity on the landscape rises nearly 610m into the air to form a great plateau that dominates the countryside for miles around. Here, legend says, the handsome Diarmuid, who had eloped with Gráinne, met his end. For sixteen years the pair had been pursued across Ireland by the aged and vengeful Finn mac Cumhaill, leader of the warrior band known as the Fianna, and the man who was to have married Gráinne. Out hunting on **Benbulben**, Finn tricked Diarmuid into fighting an enchanted boar. Diarmuid was fatally wounded and lay dying. Finn, who had the magic powers to heal him, refused to do so. In-

stead, he cut off Diarmuid's head and sent it to Gráinne, who died at the sight of it. She was carried to the caves of **Gleniff** and laid beside Diarmuid.

Carrowmore

Carrowmore is the largest megalithic cemetery in Ireland. Most are passage graves or dolmens, but because of quarrying carried out nearby some kerbstones have been lost or moved.

Drumcliff

'Under bare Ben Bulben's head' is **Drumcliff**, where William Butler Yeats is buried in his beloved Sligo, 'land of heart's desire'. Though he grew up mainly in Dublin and London, his mother came from this area and he spent many days here, roaming the countryside, listening to the stories of fishermen and farmers, and visiting at **Lissadell**, the fine Georgian house of the beautiful Constance Gore-Booth, later Countess Markievicz, the Irish revolutionary and first woman MP to Westminster. Yeats's poetry is filled with references to this landscape, while his plays *At the Hawk's Well* and *On Beltra Strand* dramatising the myths of Cúchulainn are set here.

LEITRIM

Lough Allen divides **County Leitrim** neatly in two. South of Lough Allen, the county is more water than land – with lakes and rivers interspersed with drumlins left by glaciation.

Carrick-on-Shannon

A pretty town on the river Shannon, **Carrick-on-Shannon** is devoted, not surprisingly, to boating. Here cruisers begin their trip up the **Shannon-Erne** waterways, 385 kilometres of canal, lake and river.

Parke's Castle

On the shores of Leitrim's other lake, **Lough Gill**, is the 17th century fortress built by Robert Parke. Its **courtyard** contains the foundations of an earlier tower house of an Irish chieftain Brian O'Rourke, executed for saving a shipwrecked survivor of the Spanish Armada. The stones of O'Rourke's house have been recycled into **Parke's Castle**.

Top, right, Carrick-on-Shannon, a pretty town devoted to boating, bottom, Parke's Castle on the shores of Lough Gill.

*T*he ancient province of Ulster takes in the green lakelands of **Fermanagh** and **Cavan**, the harsh boglands of **Donegal**, the ancient city of **Derry**, **Antrim** with its strange **Giant's Causeway** formation, **Belfast**, the capital of Northern Ireland, the Mournes in **Down**, the ecclesiastical city of **Armagh**, the rolling hills of **Tyrone** and the little hills of **Monaghan**.

FERMANAGH

County Fermanagh is dominated by the 80 kilometre long **Lough Erne**, which narrows to a waist at **Enniskillen** town and is dotted with wooded islands – once a string of monasteries – and Celtic and Christian monuments.

Enniskillen

At one end of Enniskillen's long main street is the castle, once the stronghold of the Maguires, at the other is the Victorian park, **Fork Hill** with its Doric column. The Maguire's fort, captured by the English in 1607, was remodelled and renamed **Enniskillen Castle**. It

Top, left, *Enniskillen, a garrison town at the neck of two lakes,* bottom, left, *the 15th century Enniskillen Castle, built in the Scottish style,* bottom, right, *a Janus stone, dating from pagan times, on Boa Island.*

Top, *the thriving fishing port of Killybegs,* middle, *Trabane Strand at Malin Beg,* bottom, *the inhospitable coast of Bloody Foreland.*

resisted attacks from the Maguires, from Jacobite forces and eventually became an 18th century barracks. The keep houses the **Heritage Centre** and the **Regimental Museum**.

Boa Island

Some of the islands that sprinkle **Lough Erne** are in fact *crannógs*, ancient manmade structures insulated from attack by water. And their presence here and the many pagan and Christian sites all around indicate early settlers. On **Boa Island** in the overgrown **Caldragh cemetery** and surrounded by early Christian tombstones, a carved *Janus* dating from pagan times stands beside the '*Lustybeg man'*, signs that pagan beliefs lived on alongside Christian ones in this isolated area.

DONEGAL

Like the remoter areas of Kerry and the west of Ireland, **Donegal** retains a strong sense of its culture and some of the finest traditional music is to be found in the *Gaeltacht* regions around **Glencolmcille** and **Bunbeg**. But it is also a place of astounding beauty with craggy mountains like **Errigal** and high moorlands, marshy lakes, and wide sweeps of sandy beaches.

This page, and facing page, *views of the awe-inspiring Grianán of Aileach, built in 1500BC and in use until the 12ᵗʰ century.*

Killybegs

Fishing is the *raison d'être* of this little town sheltered in the arm of **Killybeg's Bay. Killybegs** is the country's most successful port and its pubs and cafes are packed with fishermen from up and down the coast, especially in July when the sea anglers join them for a two week festival. At evening time, the fleet offloads its catch onto the quaysides and the locals come down to catch a bargain for dinner.

Malin Beg

One of the loveliest of golden beaches in Donegal, scooped out of a rocky inlet, **Malin Beg** has a tiny village and lies next to the awesome **Bunglass** cliffs, 610m above sea level and gleaming with mineral deposits.

Inishowen Peninsula

Pointing out into the North Sea, **Inishowen Peninsula** is almost entirely surrounded by water – **Lough Swilly** to the west and **Lough Foyle** to the east. Castles, monasteries, Christian crosses and cross slabs at **Fahan**, **Carndonagh**, **Carrowmore** and **Cooley**, but most of all the ancient fort of **Grianán of Ailech** point back to the area's rich history.

Grianán of Aileach

Built on the neck of land between the two loughs, **Grianán of Aileach** commands superb views over the northern counties.

Dating back to 1500BC, it is said to have been built by the ancient gods, and is associated with the powerful O'Neill clan from possibly the 5ᵗʰ to 12ᵗʰ century.

The Munster O'Briens dismantled it in 1101, in revenge for the destruction of their stronghold at Kincora in Clare. Each soldier was ordered to carry away a stone with him. What remains was greatly restored in the 19ᵗʰ century. The stone fort stands 23m wide with walls 4m thick inside three banks of a hill fort. Its ramparts contain chambers and walkways, connected by steps.

TYRONE

The green rolling countryside of County **Tyrone** is fertile farming land, with the **Sperrin** mountains to the north providing hikers with good walking country and bird-watchers with rich rewards. Scattered here and there are archaeological sites such as the **Beaghmore Stone Circle**. These and later traces of the inhabitants of the region are explored in two centres – the **Ulster American Folk Park** outside Omagh which looks at the history of the area's early emigrants to the United States, and the **Ulster History Park** near Gortin.

Ulster History Park

Human settlements dating back to 7000BC and all the way up to the 17th century, including a *crannóg* and a 17th century plantation town are reconstructed and explained in detail at the History Park.

Ulster History Park near Gortin: top, left, a reconstruction of a crannóg – a defensive manmade structure dating back to the time of the Celts, bottom, a reconstruction of a 17th century plantation settlement.

St Columb's Cathedral was built in 1633, though the tower dates from the Georgian era.

DERRY

Enclosed in sturdy 17th century walls, the old city of Derry climbs picturesquely up **Shipquay Street** to the **Diamond**, a market square, at the top. Outside the walls and on the opposite bank of the River Foyle, later additions sprawl up the hillside. Derry is an ancient city, named *Doire Cholmcille* ('oakwoods of Colmcille') after Saint Colmcille, the scholar, missionary and scion of a powerful northern clan, who founded a monastery here in 546AD. The settlement held a crucial point at the mouth of the Foyle, and was repeatedly attacked by Vikings and, later, the Anglo-Normans. This was the land of the powerful Gaelic chieftains, O'Neill and O'Donnell, but constant rebellion against English rule led to their lands being confiscated and the flight to the Continent in 1607. The way was open for large scale plantation of Ulster by loyal English and Scottish immigrants – and for the political divisions which still exist today. In 1613 Derry was granted to the Corporation of London, and renamed Londonderry, but today the two-thirds Catholic majority in the city tactfully uses both names. In 1688-89 came the siege of Derry when Williamite forces successfully withstood those of the Catholic King James II for fifteen weeks. In the following centuries, the linen industry boomed, and Derry's importance as a port grew.

In the past decades, Derry has been in the news again. When the civil rights movement marched in 1968, it was baton charged by the RUC – an event seen as sparking off the present phase of 'the Troubles', in 1972 Derry was the scene of infamous Bloody Sunday when British paratroopers opened fire on a crowd, and thirteen people were killed. However, Derry city council has pursued a determinedly non-sectarian policy in recent years, and Derry is surprisingly lively, with a vigorous artistic and cultural life.

St Columb's Cathedral

In the siege of Derry, this Protestant cathedral acted as battery and watch tower. The terms of surrender were catapulted in via a cannon shell, preserved in the porch. There is a tiny **museum** in the **chapter house.**

The Guildhall

Just outside the city walls on the bank of the River Foyle, stands the Guildhall which has recently been restored. Its beautiful stained glass windows illustrate the city's history.

The City Walls

Built in the 17th century, Derry's walls have never been breached which has given rise to the city's nickname of 'the maiden city'. Interspersed with bastions, now handy viewing points across the river Foyle to the **Waterside**, the **Fountain** and the **Bogside**, a complete circuit of the walls is roughly 1.6 kilometres long. Within the walls the medieval city plan is maintained – a central **Diamond** with four streets leading off to four main gateways.

Top, the Guildhall on the city quays, bottom, *Ferryquay Gate .*

Top, *strange formations on the Giant's Causeway, which imagination has wrought into 'the Chimney' and 'the Harp',* bottom, right, *the largest of the basalt formations is known as 'the Organ', for obvious reasons, this one fooled a ship of the Spanish Armada into believing it was Dunluce Castle further along the Antrim coast – and the shipwreck of the* Girona *followed.*

ANTRIM

County Antrim attracts more visitors than any other part of Northern Ireland. The **Giant's Causeway** is undoubtedly the greatest draw, but there are also stupendous views along the Antrim coastline from **Fair Head** and **Torr Head**, lengthy silver beaches backed by the sand dunes of **White Park Bay, Portstewart** and **Portrush**, and the lush glens and waterfalls of Antrim inland.

Giant's Causeway

It is difficult to believe that the **Giant's Causeway** is not manmade. A series of gigantic basalt steps, some fashioned by imaginative tour guides into features such as 'the Chimney' or 'the Harp', the formations have led to many explanatory legends. One version has Finn mac Cumhaill, leader of the warrior band known as the Fianna, building the causeway to take him across to his lover on the isle of Staffa in Scotland, where the causeway phenomenum also exists. In fact, the cause is much more pedestrian – a massive underwater explosion thousands of years ago spat out molten basalt which eventually cooled into these huge crystals.

Facing page, 'the Wishing Chair' on the Giant's Causeway.

This page, top, *the long, shallow incline of Whitepark Bay*, middle
and bottom, right, *Dunluce Castle, stronghold of the MacDonnell
clan, sits perilously close to the edge of the Antrim coast.*

Whitepark Bay

West along the coast from the **Giant's Causeway** is a
very different scene – a long curve of white sand,
Whitepark Bay, backed by grassy dunes and in the
dip of two of them, a tiny church, said to be the
smallest in Ireland.

Dunluce Castle

Clinging to a rock on the edge of the sea, **Dunluce
Castle** is a vast ruin. Claimed by fearless Sorley Boy
MacDonnell in the mid-16th century, it was reinforced
with cannon from the *Girona*, a Spanish Armada ves-
sel wrecked nearby, embellished with an elegant log-
gia – unique in Ireland – and a manor house, of
which the shell remains. In 1639 a banquet was inter-
rupted when part of the castle collapsed into the sea,
taking with it both the servants and the dinner. A
huge cave pierces the cliffside below the castle, and
the howling of the waves against the rock in stormy
weather may explain the spectre of the 'banshee that
sweeps the tower floor'.

Bushmills Whiskey Distillery

The picturebook town of **Bushmills** owes its fame to the whiskey distilled there. In business since 1608, the Old Bushmills Distillery is the oldest legal distillery in the world. Traditionally, visitors to the Giant's Causeway would stop off to refresh themselves with a few measures. Unlike Scotch whiskey Bushmills malt is distilled three times which gives it a smoother flavour, but visitors to the plant can decide for themselves as the tour ends with a generous tot.

Nº4 · Nº2 · Nº3 WASH STI

Ballintoy

From the east end of **Whitepark Bay**, a footpath leads to **Ballintoy** harbour, a limestone breakwater, filled with fishermen who can be persuaded to take visitors to the islands; or along the coastline to inspect **Dunluce Castle** and its cave; or to **Sheep's Island**, that strange skyscraper of rock a kilometre offshore and topped with a grassy carpet that is home to a cormorant colony; or to **Carrick-a-rede**, an outcrop of rock connected to land by a rope bridge.

Carrick-a-rede

There is a salmon farm on the southeast side of **Carrick-a-rede** island and has been for at least 350 years. The outcrop itself stands in the path of Atlantic salmon returning home to spawn in the rivers – Carrick-a-rede means 'Rock in the Road'.

Originally the rope bridge spanned the gap between the island and the Antrim coast from April to September so that fishermen could access the island during the salmon season, and a print dating from 1790 shows a rope bridge then in place. But these days it seems more popular with the visitors who enjoy swinging above the sheer drop on the 24m long bouncing rope bridge.

Carrick-a-rede rope bridge joins a salmon fishery on the rocky island to the mainland. As soon as you set foot on the 24m long rope-and-plank bridge it bounces and sways.

Top, *Torr Head, from here Scotland is only nineteen kilometres away,* middle, left, *a long vista along the Antrim coastline near Runabay Head ,* bottom, *Cushendun village in the Glens of Antrim is preserved by the National Trust.*

Torr Head

The **Antrim coastline** is spectacular, running out to sea in headlands, dipping into rocky bays, rising again to rough moorland covered in heather and ferns. At **Torr Head**, the **Mull of Kintyre** in **Scotland** is only nineteen kilometres away, and it is said that until recently Protestants would row across to church there. Further west at **Fair Head**, where the narrow road zigzags upwards to jagged cliffs, 183m high, the islands of Scotland are clearly visible across the straits. There are three lakes behind the cliffs, one of which, **Lough na Cranagh**, contains a manmade island called a *crannóg* – also found in **Lough Erne** in **Fermanagh**. Another, called **Loughareema**, is known as the 'vanishing lake' – it floods and then disappears into the porous limestone beneath.

The Glens of Antrim

The nine **Glens of Antrim** are famous for their beauty – and the legends that are attached. In **Glenaan**, on the slopes of **Tievebulliagh** mountain where Stone Age chippings for axe heads have been found, is the tomb of Ossian, son of Finn mac Cumhaill the warrior, and the greatest Celtic poet. The other glens are **Glentaisie**, **Glenshesk**, **Glendun**, the 'brown glen', **Glenballyeamon**, **Glenariff** with its wonderful waterfalls, **Glencloy** and **Glenarm**.

Glenarm

The southernmost of the glens, **Glenarm** is home to the earls of Antrim, descendants of Sorley Boy Mac-Donnell of **Dunluce Castle**. In 1603 Sorley Boy's son, Randal, built a hunting lodge here. Later this was enlarged into the castle which was rebuilt in 1817 to include Gothic, Tudor and Jacobean features as well as Dutch gables.

The town grew up around the industry of stone quarrying, and limestone and chalk leave the port, while salmon is farmed very successfully here.

Carnlough

Sitting at the head of **Glencloy**, the village of **Carnlough** used to depend for its income on the export of limestone quarried in the hills behind. In fact, most of the village seems to be built of the bright white stone, even the harbour has a clocktower and courthouse of limestone. Now the renovated harbour is a port of call for yachtsmen, anglers and trawlers offloading lobster and crab.

Carrickfergus

The massive Anglo-Norman castle of **Carrickfergus** was begun by John de Courcy in 1180s to guard the entrance to Belfast Lough. However, it was soon captured by Hugh de Lacy and much of it built as it stands today. In 1315, now the property of the crown, the castle and a beleaguered garrison withstood a year-long siege by eating the bodies of eight of their unfortunate Scottish prisoners. After many other historical twists, the castle was retaken for the crown in 1690. Now, restored to its original state, it is open to the public.

Following pages, Carnlough Bay on the beautiful Antrim coast.

Top right, and bottom, left, *salmon farming in Glenarm,* middle, *the harbour at Carnlough,* bottom, right, *Carrickfergus Castle on the north of Belfast Lough has changed hands many times.*

BELFAST

Six of the nine counties of the ancient province of Ulster form modern Northern Ireland and are part of the United Kingdom – Derry, Tyrone, Antrim, Fermanagh, Down and Armagh. **Belfast** is the capital of Northern Ireland and sits in the valley of the **Lagan River** where it pours into a wide sea lough. To the north and west the **Black Mountain**, **Cave Hill** and **Divis Mountain** rise, while to the south the Castlereagh Hills slope gently towards **County Down**. The city of Belfast developed comparatively late. The 17th century brought French Huguenot refugees with skills that boosted the linen industry and, together with shipbuilding, brought the city great prosperity during the following centuries. Belfast has been less fortunate this century – much of the city was bombed in the Second World War, while the Troubles have also left their mark and, apart from its Victorian centre, Belfast is largely a modern city.

City Hall

The grand solid rectangle of City Hall dominates the centre of Belfast. Built by the city fathers in 1888 when Queen Victoria granted Belfast the status of a city, it was completed in 1906 and is a fine example of Victorian pomp. Ironically, the young Londoner Alfred Brumwell Thomas who designed this monument to civic pride had to sue the city fathers for payment. The Hall sits squarely around a central courtyard with its 52m high dome forming a landmark for visitors.

This page, top, left, *City Hall with its 52m high dome dominates the centre of Belfast,* bottom, left, *the Grand Staircase – a monument to civic pride.*

Donegall Square

City Hall is surrounded by the grand Victorian architecture of **Donegall Square**, with the Scottish Provident building notable for its exuberant stonework. A Venetian-style building, once a linen warehouse, is now occupied by Marks & Spencer, while the **Linen Hall Library**, the city's public library also fronts onto Donegall Square.

Top, right and bottom, City Hall sits in the middle of Donegall Square with its commemorative statutary, surrounded by fine buildings dating from its Victorian heyday.

Albert Memorial Clock Tower

One of the reasons that Belfast developed so slowly as a city was that much of its land was prone to flooding, and very marshy – a bad foundation for building. Piles 9 to 12m long had to be driven into the bedrock to support the larger buildings in the docklands. The **Albert Memorial Clock Tower** – a mini 'Big Ben' standing at the docks end of **High Street** – has suffered from this and dips more than a metre to one side. It was designed by W J Barre, an exponent of the exuberant neo-Gothic style, in 1867 and features a statue of Queen Victoria's consort, Prince Albert.

Left, *the striking landmark of the Albert Clock stands at the dockland end of High Street and commemorates,* below, *Prince Albert, Queen Victoria's consort.*

Top and middle, *Queen's University designed by Sir Charles Lanyon mimics the Tudor style,* bottom, right, *the Palm House in the Botanic Gardens, one of the finest and earliest examples of curvilinear glass and ironwork.*

Queen's University

Queen's University is set back from the street at one end of **'the Golden Mile'**, a stretch of restaurants and pubs that runs from **Great Victoria Street** past the university and on to **Malone Road**. Designed by Sir Charles Lanyon who was responsible for many of the public and commercial building in Belfast, and modelled on Magdelen College in Oxford, it presents a Tudor-style front in mellow yellow brick and dates from 1849.

Botanic Gardens

Close by Queen's University are the **Botanic Gardens,** opened in 1827, with many quiet walkways and rose gardens. The **Palm House** is a glorious blend of curved glass and cast iron, again designed by Sir Charles Lanyon and built by a Dublin iron founder, Richard Turner. It is filled with rare tropical plants, some of which are over a hundred years old and was the model for the Palm House in Kew Gardens in London. The **Ulster Museum** fronts onto the gardens.

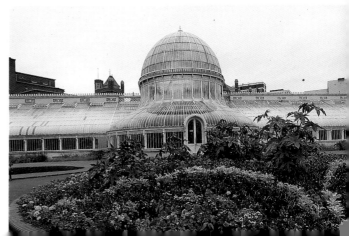

Crown Liquor Saloon

Belfast is known for its fantastic Victorian and Edwardian pubs, such as the **Morning Star** in Pottinger's Entry, the **Elephant Bar** in Upper North Street, but the most flamboyant is the **Crown Liquor Saloon** on Great Victoria Street. Built in 1885 by Patrick Flanagan, it shows the influence of his travels in Spain and Italy. It has stained glass, elaborate Victorian mouldings, delightful panelled snugs lit by gas light and equipped with a bell to call the barman. The Crown suffered from the many bomb blasts that shook the Europa Hotel opposite. In 1981 the National Trust, who now own the bar, carried out meticulous renovations and it is once more a wonderful place to sip a pint of Guinness and sample Strangford Lough's oysters.

Top, left, the Crown Liquor Saloon dates from the 1880s and is extravagantly ornate both outside and, bottom, *inside.*

Pottinger's Entry

The narrow passageways leading off **High Street** and **Ann Street** are known as 'entries' and lead to some of the best pubs – the **Morning Star** is in **Pottinger's Entry**, while Belfast's oldest pub, **White's Tavern**, is in **Wine Cellar Entry** and the **Globe** is in **Joy's Entry.**

The Europa Hotel

The **Europa** has earned the unhappy reputation of being the most bombed building in Europe. Nonetheless, last renovated in 1994, it is now *the* place to be seen drinking, and celebrities visiting Belfast invariably opt to stay here.

Stormont

The former Northern Ireland parliament was housed in **Stormont**, a sober neo-classical mansion, opened in 1932 by the Prince of Wales. Designed by Sir Arnold Thornley in the Portland stone that graces City Hall, it stands on granite quarried from the Mourne mountains. It ends a mile-long avenue in the middle of parklands, 9.6 kilometres east of Belfast.

Top, right, Pottinger's Entry is just one of the narrow passageways off High Street, most conceal fine pubs, bottom left, the Europa Hotel has earned an unfortunate reputation as the most bombed hotel in Europe, bottom right, Parliament Buildings, Stormont, east of Belfast, a mile-long avenue leads up to its fine white portico.

Political murals

Like Derry, Belfast has many political murals in its working-class areas. In **West Belfast** Catholic murals on the **Falls Road**, **Shaw's Road** and **Beechmont Avenue** depict scenes from the 1845-48 famine, the personification of '*Saoirse*' or 'Freedom' and other symbols of Republicanism. The Protestant tradition of mural painting is significantly different with less complex symbolism such as flags, slogans or the Red Hand of Ulster, though occasionally King Billy astride his white horse at the Battle of the Boyne appears. These are to be found on the **Shankill** and **Crumlin roads** and along **Sandy Row**.

Facing page, top, *Mount Stewart House was home to the infamous Viscount Castlereagh*, middle, right, *'Hambletonian' by George Stubbs*, bottom, left, *the dining room at Mount Stewart with a set of Empire chairs used by the delegates to the Congress of Vienna in 1815.*

This page, top, and middle row, *Catholic murals painted on gable ends and*, bottom, left and right, *loyalist murals.*

DOWN

The flat green countryside of the **Ards peninsula** in **County Down** embraces the huge expanse of **Strangford Lough** where St Patrick made his first landfall. It is an area rich in prehistoric remains and early Christian sites such as those at **Inch Abbey** and **Grey Abbey**, as well as the grand country estates of **Castle Ward House** and **Rowallane**. Further south the jagged **Mourne Mountains** mark the border with the Republic of Ireland.

Mount Stewart House

Mount Stewart House is famous for being the seat of Viscount Castlereagh, who was largely responsible for bringing about the Act of Union of 1800 which amalgamated the Irish Parliament with that of Westminster. The house was built in the 1740s overlooking Strangford Lough, with additions in the early 19th century.

Mount Stewart possesses one of the most famous paintings in Ireland, 'Hambletonian' by George Stubbs. The racehorse is shown being rubbed down by a groom after it won at Newmarket in 1799. The diningroom contains twenty-two Empire chairs used by the delegates to the Congress of Vienna in 1815 – the chairbacks and seats depict the coat of arms of each delegate and the nation they represent.

But it is the gardens that steal the show. Apart from the stunning **Temple of the Winds**, a banqueting hall built over the lough in 1780s, there are the formal gardens laid out in the 1920s. Warmed by an unusually humid microclimate, the garden's rare plants grow at a phenomenal rate.

Newcastle

At the base of **Slieve Donard** mountain, the highest peak in the Mourne range, and nestled among the foothills of the Mourne Mountains, **Newcastle** is a booming seaside resort and a good base from which to explore the mountains and parks that surround it. Its sandy curve of a beach, swimming pools, adventure centres and famous ice cream parlour make it a paradise for children.

Greencastle

This ruined fort on the north side of **Carlingford Lough** gazes at its fellow sentinel **Carlingford Castle** on the other shore. Both were built at roughly the same time in the 13th century. Entrusted to the de Burghs, earls of Ulster, by the Crown, **Greencastle** came under attack many times from the Irish. It was around the time that Gerald, 8th earl of Kildare, was granted the castle as a reward for quelling a rebellion in 1505, that the castle was enlarged. When he fell from favour the castle was granted together with its sister fortress Carlingford Castle to Sir Nicholas Bagnall in 1552. He made it suitable for his family – replacing the arrow slits with large windows, and adding a fireplace. It is now state-owned.

Top, left, *the seaside resort of Newcastle is overshadowed by Slieve Donard, the highest of the Mourne mountain range,* and bottom, *Greencastle, a 13th century ruined fortress that guards the north side of Carlingford Lough.*

Top, *view of the Mourne Mountains – a wild range of granite peaks often obscured by mists, which shelters the Silent Valley reservoir, the source of Belfast's water, and scattered here and there isolated cottages,* bottom, right, *the famous Mourne Wall.*

The Mourne Mountains

The Mourne Mountains stretch from **Newcastle** south and west to **Carlingford Lough**. Great granite hills, they started life 65 million years ago when masses of molten rock thrust upwards through the earth. Now they are covered in upland heath – which is vivid with heather and gorse – and, to the south of the range, grassland which yields a wide range of flowering plants. In certain pockets, old woods of hazel, birch and holly stand, while in others, there are state plantations of conifer. The isolated cliffs and crags of the Mournes offer important nesting sites for birds of prey and peregrine falcons, buzzards and kestrels have been sighted here.

One of the outstanding manmade features of the Mournes is the **Mourne Wall**. It is a dry stone wall like those found in the Aran Islands, and uses no lime mortar to hold its boulders together. The stone mason's skill and careful choice of stone are the ingredients for these deceptively sturdy but delicately balanced walls. At 35.2 kilometres in length, and running over all the highest peaks in the Mourne range, the Mourne Wall is one of the most spectacular examples of

This page, top, *the patchwork of small fields bound by dry stone walls is reminiscent of the west of Ireland.* Bottom, left, *heathers, gorse and broom bring the high moorland of the Mourne Mountains alive with colour.*

Facing page, top, *the Silent Valley tucked into the peaks of the Mourne Mountains.*

dry stone walling in Ireland. It is built of cut granite, laid up to a height of 2.4m, and took eighteen years to construct.

Locals describe the Mournes as 'shy' because they are so often hidden in the clouds that catch on their peaks and so are rarely to be seen. But that does not discourage the hill-walkers who come to this area. Hikers love the slow climb up these crags and the splendid views on a clear day from the top. None of the climbs is too arduous – the highest peak, **Slieve Donard**, is 852m. One of the finest walks in the range begins behind the seaside town of **Annalong** and goes to the dam at **Ben Crom** above the **Silent Valley**, a huge reservoir that provides the water for Belfast city. From Ben Crom, you can see the countryside spread out in each direction – inland to the hilly country of Armagh, south across Carlingford Lough, northwards to Belfast and beyond, or out across the sea.

This page, top, left, *Armagh is sited, like Rome, among seven hills,* top, right, *Navan Fort dates from 2000BC and is believed to be the site of legendary Emain Macha, the capital of Ulster and court of the heroic Red Branch knights.*

Facing page, *the Catholic Cathedral of St Patrick in Armagh city.*

ARMAGH

Famous as the ecclesiastical capital of Ireland – both the Catholic and Anglican faiths have their headquarters here – and rich in history, Armagh is nevertheless a surprisingly compact town. Perched on its hilltops or tucked into its streets are two cathedrals, a planetarium, a library rich in first editions and rare books and an elegant Georgian mall, while some miles outside Armagh are the older remains of the mythic Navan Fort.

Catholic St Patrick's Cathedral

Armagh is closely associated with St Patrick, Ireland's patron saint. Having sailed into Strangford Lough, he made his landfall at Down and was believed to have founded his first church in Armagh in 445AD on the hill where the Church of Ireland cathedral now stands. From outside, the Catholic cathedral seems ordinary enough, another 19th century neo-Gothic church set on a slight hill. But a glance into the large and spacious interior reveals a dazzling rich mosaic masterpiece.

Navan Fort

Once the grass-covered mound of **Navan Fort** was, it is believed, **Emain Macha**, the ancient capital of **Ulster**. Here the *Red Branch Knights* were based with their great warrior Cúchulainn, who died defending Ulster. It is thought they reigned here until 332AD when Navan Fort was razed to the ground and the knights were vanquished into the wilds of Down and north to Antrim. Their heroic deeds, passed on for centuries by word of mouth, survive in the stories of the *Ulster Cycle*.

INDEX

Map of Ireland .... page 2
Introduction .... " 3

DUBLIN .... " 11
Around Dublin .... " 40
Around O'Connell Street .... " 34
Brazen Head Pub .... " 26
Christ Church Cathedral .... " 23
City Hall .... " 22
College Green .... " 22
Custom House .... " 32
Dame Street .... " 22
Dublin Castle .... " 20
Dublin Writers' Museum .... " 35
Fitzwilliam Street .... " 19
Four Courts .... " 33
Garden of Remembrance .... " 38
General Post Office .... " 31
Grafton Street .... " 17
Grand Canal .... " 39
Guinness Storehouse .... " 28
Hugh Lane Municipal Gallery .... " 35
Kilmainham Gaol .... " 29
King's Inns .... " 36
Leinster House .... " 17
Liffey, The .... " 31
Mansion House .... " 16
Marsh's Library .... " 29
Merrion Square .... " 19
National Gallery, The .... " 16
National Library, The .... " 15
O'Connell Bridge .... " 31
Parnell Square .... " 36
Phoenix Park .... " 38
Royal Hospital Kilmainham .... " 29
St Audoen's Church .... " 24
St Michan's Church .... " 33
St Patrick's Cathedral .... " 25
St Stephen's Green .... " 18
Temple Bar .... " 26
Trinity College .... " 12
Trinity Library .... " 14

CONNAUGHT .... " 86
Aran Islands .... " 92
Ballinasloe October Fair .... " 89
Benbulben .... " 96
Boyle Abbey .... " 95
Browne Doorway .... " 87
Carrick-on-Shannon .... " 97
Carrowmore .... " 96
Clifden .... " 90
Cong Abbey .... " 94
Drumcliff .... " 96
Dun Aenghus .... " 92
Dunguaire Castle .... " 91
Galway .... " 86
Galway International Oyster Festival ... " 88
Inishmore .... " 92
Kylemore Abbey .... " 90
Leitrim .... " 97
Long Walk, The .... " 87

Lough Corrib .... page 91
Lynch's Castle .... " 87
Mayo .... " 93
Parke's Castle .... " 97
Roscommon .... " 95
Ross Errilly Abbey .... " 91
Sligo .... " 96
Spanish Arch .... " 87
LEINSTER .... " 42
Bective Abbey .... " 57
Birr .... " 56
Browne's Hill Dolmen .... " 51
Carlow .... " 51
Castletown House .... " 54
Clonmacnois Monastery .... " 55
Drogheda .... " 60
Glendalough .... " 44
Hill of Tara .... " 58
Hook Head .... " 47
Irish National Stud .... " 53
Japanese Gardens .... " 53
Jerpoint Abbey .... " 50
Kildare .... " 52
Kilkenny .... " 49
Kilkenny Castle .... " 49
Kilmore Quay .... " 47
Louth .... " 60
Meath .... " 57
Mellifont Abbey .... " 60
Muiredach's Cross .... " 61
Newgrange .... " 59
Offaly .... " 55
St Brigid's Cathedral .... " 52
Thatched Cottages .... " 48
Trim Castle .... " 57
Wexford .... " 46
Wicklow .... " 43
MUNSTER .... " 62
Adare .... " 79
Aillwee Caves .... " 84
Ballyvaughan .... " 83
Bantry House .... " 71
Barleycove Beach .... " 70
Bunratty Castle .... " 80
Burren, The .... " 82
Clare .... " 80
Cliffs of Moher .... " 80
Cobh Village .... " 66
Conor Pass .... " 77
Cork .... " 65
Cork City .... " 65
Cork City Gaol .... " 66
Dingle Village .... " 76
Doolin .... " 83
Doolin Pier .... " 84
Drombeg Stone Circle .... " 69
Dunbeg Fort .... " 78
Gallarus Oratory, The .... " 78
Garnish Island .... " 72
Inch .... " 77
Kenmare .... " 74
Kerry .... " 73
Kilmakedar Church .... " 78

King John's Castle .... page 79
Kinsale .... " 68
Lakes of Killarney .... " 75
Limerick .... " 79
Lisdoonvarna .... " 83
Lough Gur .... " 79
Mizen Head .... " 70
Old Courthouse, The .... " 68
Poulnabrone Dolmen .... " 82
Reginald's Tower .... " 63
Rock of Cashel .... " 62
Seal Island .... " 72
St Multose Church .... " 68
Timoleague Abbey .... " 67
Tipperary .... " 62
Waterford .... " 63
Waterford Crystal Factory .... " 64
ULSTER .... " 98
Albert Memorial Clock Tower .... " 116
Antrim .... " 105
Armagh .... " 126
Ballintoy .... " 109
Belfast .... " 114
Boa Island .... " 99
Botanic Gardens .... " 117
Bushmills Whiskey Distillery .... " 108
Carnlough .... " 111
Carrick-a-rede .... " 109
Carrickfergus .... " 111
Catholic St Patrick's Cathedral .... " 126
City Hall .... " 114
City Walls (Derry), The .... " 104
Crown Liquor Saloon .... " 118
Derry .... " 103
Donegal .... " 99
Donegall Square .... " 115
Down .... " 121
Dunluce Castle .... " 107
Enniskillen .... " 98
Europa Hotel .... " 119
Fermanagh .... " 98
Giant's Causeway .... " 105
Glenarm .... " 111
Glens of Antrim, The .... " 110
Greencastle .... " 122
Grianán of Aileach .... " 100
Guildhall (Derry) .... " 104
Inishowen Peninsula .... " 100
Killybegs .... " 100
Malin Beg .... " 100
Mount Stewart House .... " 121
Mourne Mountains, The .... " 123
Navan Fort .... " 126
Newcastle .... " 122
Political Murals .... " 120
Pottinger's Entry .... " 119
Queen's University .... " 117
St Columb's Cathedral .... " 103
Stormont .... " 119
Torr Head .... " 110
Tyrone .... " 102
Ulster History Park .... " 102
Whitepark Bay .... " 107

Project and editorial conception: Casa Editrice Bonechi
Publication Manager: Monica Bonechi
Cover, picture research, graphic design and Make-up: Sonia Gottardo
Map: Studio Grafico Daniela Mariani, Pistoia
Editing: Anna Baldini

Text: Frances Power

© Copyright by Casa Editrice Bonechi, Via Cairoli 18/b, 50131 Florence, Italy.
E-mail: bonechi@bonechi.it - Internet: www.bonechi.it
ISBN 88-8029-768-6

Photographs from archives of Casa Editrice Bonechi taken by Ghigo Roli.
Photographs on page 102 by courtesy of The Ulster History Park.
Photographs on page 28 (top and bottom middle) courtesy of the Guinness Storehouse and on page 30 (bottom right) courtesy of Emma Byrne.